POETRY OF WAR
1939–1945

Poetry of War
1939–1945

Edited by Ian Hamilton

NEW ENGLISH LIBRARY
TIMES MIRROR

First published in Great Britain by Alan Ross Ltd.

*

FIRST NEL PAPERBACK EDITION NOVEMBER 1972

*

NEL Books are published by
New English Library Limited from Barnard's Inn, Holborn, London, E.C.1.
Made and printed in Great Britain by Hunt Barnard Printing Ltd., Aylesbury, Bucks.

45001320 0

Contents

7 – History's Thread

8 – The Americans

9 – Some Autobiographical Statements

Introduction

'It is impossible to indict a whole poetic decade, wrote Kenneth Allott in 1948, but he was surely optimistic. The decade in which he wrote this, the now notorious Forties, has been thoroughly written off in most current pigeon-holings of contemporary verse as a period dominated by the rhetoric of the New Apocalypse and by a war-time hysteria that could only have produced an 'impossibly overblown, exaggerated, strained' reaction from its poets. With war finally declared, we are told, the issues were suddenly private and absolute; in the general chaos it was impossible to maintain not only the clinical admonitory stance of the Thirties poets but also their precision and intelligence. Rhetoric fell naturally to the uniquely inspired seer, communication was just another of the egalitarian lies. In the words of G. S. Fraser, introducing the 1941 anthology, *The White Horseman* (ed. J. F. Hendry and Henry Treece):

> The obscurity of our poetry, its air of something desperately snatched from dream or woven round a chime of words, are the results of disintegration, not in ourselves, but in society.

And this is the sort of typical Forties reflex poem that he was defending:

> Crow, wooden lightning, from a sky of thorn
> O cross-ribbed Adam, tumbled hill of blood.
> While blinded shell and body's thunder churn
> Ear to worm-ball, tongue to lipless stone.

The Forties did of course produce hundreds of poems of this calibre and too many of them were lavishly overpraised at the time, but to take this kind of thing – to be in the least a typical or necessary response to the 'impossible conditions' of the Second World War is a cruel distortion. It is one of the purposes of this anthology to make this clear, to do justice to those poets who did not rush to extremes, whose work, in direct descent from Eliot and Auden, attempted to confront a disintegrating world in personal terms that could make poetic sense out of it. There is perhaps more honest effort than distinct achievement in most of the poems which are here anthologized, but that is only to be expected of any decade; what matters is that we get a more accurate picture of what, in general, poets of the time were trying to do.

'Acceptance seems so spiritless, protest so vain. In between the two I live', wrote Alun Lewis, and it was this attentive, ambivalent note, rather than a hectoring, panicky display of godheads, that was truly characteristic of the time. To poets like Lewis, Keith Douglas, Roy Fuller, the problem was to give a real practical meaning to Fraser's parenthesis above, 'not in ourselves'. There is certainly in their work despair at the brittle systems, the empires breaking like biscuits, but what one admires as much as anything else is their determination to be sane in spite of all this; that is to say, to be articulate and intelligible, a sensitive participant, and to be scrupulous with the language. These are the qualities which I have tried to represent in my selection.

Alex Comfort has described his generation as one that grew up 'from early adolescence in the almost complete certainty that we should be killed in action', a generation brought up on grisly remembrances of 1914–18, on rumours from Spain, the accelerating menace of Nazi Germany, the imminent, and mostly desired, collapse of the capitalist system, and so on; they came to war knowing more or less what it would be like but never sure that it was worth it. 'We have all' wrote Comfort, 'adopted one or another goal – death or refusal'. One might prefer to say that the active-service poet felt himself to have been forcibly adopted by both; a recurrent theme is the threat to the poet's personal identity that was posed by their interpenetration. Depersonalized by the inevitability of death, he was at the same time made acutely aware of his responsibilities – as an artist – in the practical effort of refusal.

Certainly it was impossible to recapture either the heroic or the fiercely anti-propagandist note of the poet of the First World War. Few romantic illusions could be nourished by what often seemed to be a contest between machines and ants; the war was too fragmentary, haphazard, too largely an affair of training camps, troopships, YMCA hostels, incessant bullshit and insufferable redtape. The rituals of Army life seemed merely to perpetuate the class-system which many hoped this war would finally do away with. To be shrewd, accurately observant and self-aware; this was one way of coping with a dreary, pointless and intermittently brutal interruption of the personal allegiances that really mattered, and a certain integrity could be guaranteed by knowing that one had seen through the 'cheat' practised by the generals and bankers, the 'guff' disseminated by the propaganda machines. 'We do not wish to moralize, only to ease our dusty throats,' wrote Donald Bain, and this was a typical feeling; the generalizations had all been made and they were almost certainly all false; ideas as well as myths were helpless now – it was a question of survival and sanity in the face of what seemed to be an irreparable corruption of human nature, the 'end of history's thread'. A direct eye, an honest precision of language, a vitality of the imagination – these were worth fostering and protecting. As Henry Reed put it:

> Things may be the same again; and we must fight
> Not in the hope of winning but rather of keeping
> Something alive.

Where Wilfred Owen could write that 'All a poet can do today is warn and confidently assume a central, spokesmanlike role,' a poet like Keith Douglas was merely able to reflect: 'To be sentimental or emotional now is dangerous to oneself and to others. To trust anyone or to admit to any hope of a better world is criminally foolish as it is to stop working for it.' Owen, of course, could envisage an audience that needed to be stirred into a realization of what modern war was about, an audience either innocent, complacent or corrupt, and one well-used to being lulled by the kind of volunteer patriotics which the Conscription Act had made not only impossible but unnecessary to entice from the poet of the Second World War. The isolation that the First World War poet felt from his audience was expressed in the Second World War as the isolation that, say, the British officer felt from the Indian peasant, the African landscape, or that the poet soldier felt from his fellow-soldiers; his civilian audience was very often having a worse time than he was, and although Robert Graves was almost certainly indulging himself when he wrote that the soldier of 1939–45 had lived on the whole a far safer life than the munition maker who in the First World War was despised as a shirker, it was clearly true that there were few grounds on which the soldier poet could feel that his noble function was to warn, awaken or inform. To imagine, in any case, that this was the crucial function of war poetry was to make the mistake of poets like the Apocalyptic leader, Henry Treece, who, believing that poetry should 'prevent such horrors for the future' found himself with nothing to write about as soon as he was called up. The poems in this book are not likely to prevent – at least, not in the direct, medicinal way that Treece seemed to require – any of our own future horrors, and they are all the more valuable, I think, because nobody pretended that they would.

The poets represented in this anthology were all members of the Armed Services at one time or another during the 1939–45 war, and the poems have been separated into what seem the most significant broad categories of subject matter. There is always a certain artificiality in this kind of division, but it seems appropriate here and it has been done sparingly. A brief selection of war poems from Americans has been added, but more as a useful side-glance than anything in the least definitive.

I am particularly pleased to be able to include a series of prose statements from a number of the poets themselves; I trust that these will compensate for whatever seems too literary and speculative in my own approach to the period these poets lived through.

Ian Hamilton

1—'Simplify me when I'm dead'

Keith Douglas

Canoe

Well, I am thinking this may be my last
summer, but cannot lose even a part
of pleasure in the old-fashioned art of
idleness. I cannot stand aghast

at whatever doom hovers in the background;
while grass and buildings and the somnolent river,
who know they are allowed to last for ever,
exchange between them the whole subdued sound

of this hot time. What sudden fearful fate
can deter my shade wandering next year
from a return? Whistle and I will hear
and come another evening, when this boat

travels with you alone towards Iffley;
as you lie looking up for thunder again,
this cool touch does not betoken rain;
it is my spirit that kisses your mouth lightly.

Alun Lewis

Autumn, 1939

The beech boles whiten in the swollen stream;
Their red leaves, shaken from the creaking boughs,
Float down the flooded meadow, half in dream,
Seen in a mirror cracked by broken vows,

Water-logged, slower, deeper, swirling down
Between the indifferent hills who also saw
Old jaundiced knights jog listlessly to town
To fight for love in some unreal war.

Black leaves are piled against the roaring weir;
Dark closes round the manor and the hut;
The dead knight moulders on his rotting bier,
And one by one the warped old casements shut.

Bernard Gutteridge

In September 1939

The last war was my favourite picture story.
Illustrated London News bound in the study;
The German baynonet we believed still bloody

But was just rusty. Privacy of death.
My uncle's uniform meant more than glory;
Surprise that grief should be so transitory ...

All the predictions of adolescence had
Disposed of glory in their realist path:
There'd be no need to duck and hold your breath.

Now, looking as useless and as beautiful
As dragonflies, the plump silver balloons
Hang over London also like zany moons.

Yet from the blacked-out windows death still seems
Private, not an affair that's shared by all
The distant people, the flats, the Town Hall.

But some remember Spain and the black spots
They shouted 'Bombers' at. That memory screams
That we know as a film or in bad dreams.

Fear will alight on each like a dunce's cap
Or an unguessed disease unless death drops
Quicker than the sirens or the traffic stops.

Drummond Allison

The Cold Thoughts

Oh! cold as any snowfruit, colder than
Compulsory bathing or some smiling Head
Master, untouched these thoughts have lately lain
Along the scalloped edges of the brain
Colder than greens long-left upon a red
Enamel plate. But now the Baker Man
Warms up the engine of his different van
– Now round and numbered is the noisy bread
Of war he must distribute – and in vain
Warns us of what we were: the sticks who ran,
The flying child, the optimistic dead,
All those cold thoughts are steaming now again.
For every morning then the bullfinch woke us
Boasting about his berries, or the persian
Scratched at the door. We saw the huge arriving
Grocers and guests and ghosts, we saw them leaving.
Sun served a fault or chose his old incursion
To crowd the net, changed ends, as if to make us
Nervous, to try at last his hocus-pocus
Among those dark spectators (whose impassion
Forgave the crocuses their annual waving)
The yews themselves and larches. Till the raucous
Leghorns were quiet, the bats made full confession,
Christ and the bogey made their dangerous living.

I'm lost and losing and about to lose,
My mind like some forgotten frigidaire
After a party empty and the switch
Still on. And that verandah and deep ditch
Of dock and trampled nettle, landings where
Waits and the giggling girls and hoovers whose
Voices are stolen bore their witness; whose
Loss is announced at last! But darling where
We watched the yellow night, the losing which
Evicts all others occupied me there.
Lost God and garden (with their broken rose-
Trellises) need not ask each other which

Defeat has beaten theirs, what beauty those
– With love so obvious and why and whose.
So sorrow casts out sorrow, minus times
Minus makes plus. The truthful are running
Across the minefields of my fear, and I
Can trace and follow them tonight. Though by
Fast flare and Verey light I see the tombs
Of what my cold thoughts killed or what my darling
Had put to death by tolerance, I say:
'Synchronize watches, we are going dancing, are advancing,
Spite of the blinded windows and the jaundice of the Thames.'

Sidney Keyes

Elegy (*In Memoriam S.K.K.*)

April again and it is a year again
Since you walked out and slammed the door
Leaving us tangled in your words. Your brain
Lives in the bankbook, and your eyes look up
Laughing from the carpet on the floor.
And we still drink from your silver cup.

It is a year again since they poured
The dumb ground into your mouth:
And yet we know, by some recurring word
Or look caught unawares, that you still drive
Our thoughts like the smart cobs of your youth –
When you and the world were alive.

A year again, and we have fallen on bad times
Since they gave you to the worms.
I am ashamed to take delight in these rhymes
Without grief; but you need no tears.
We shall never forget nor escape you, nor make terms
With your enemies, the swift-devouring years.

Alun Lewis

The Sentry

I have begun to die.
For now at last I know
That there is no escape
From Night. Not any dream
Nor breathless images of sleep
Touch my bat's-eyes. I hang
Leathery-arid from the hidden roof
Of Night, and sleeplessly
I watch within Sleep's province.
I have left
The lovely bodies of the boy and girl
Deep in each other's placid arms;
And I have left
The beautiful lanes of sleep
That barefoot lovers follow to this last
Cold shore of thought I guard.
I have begun to die
And the guns' implacable silence
Is my black interim, my youth and age,
In the flower of fury, the folded poppy,
Night.

Charles Causley

Song of the Dying Gunner A.A.1

Oh mother my mouth is full of stars
As cartridges in the tray
My blood is a twin-branched scarlet tree
And it runs all runs away.

Oh *Cooks to the Galley* is sounded off
And the lads are down in the mess
But I lie by the forrard gun
With a bullet in my breast.

Don't send me a parcel at Christmas time
Of socks and nutty and wine
And don't depend on a long weekend
By the Great Western Railway line.

Farewell, Aggie Weston, the Barracks at Guz,
Hang my tiddley suit on the door
I'm sewn up neat in a canvas sheet
And I shan't be home no more.

Keith Douglas

On a Return from Egypt

To stand here in the wings of Europe
disheartened, I have come away
from the sick land where in the sun lay
the gentle sloe-eyed murderers
of themselves, exquisite under a curse;
here to exercise my depleted fury.

For the heart is a coal, growing colder
when jewelled cerulean seas change
into grey rocks, grey water-fringe,
sea and sky altering like a cloth
till colour and sheen are gone both:
cold is an opiate of the soldier.

And all my endeavours are unlucky explorers
come back, abandoning the expedition;
the specimens, the lilies of ambition
still spring in their climate, still unpicked:
but time, time is all I lacked
to find them, as the great collectors before me.

The next month, then, is a window
and with a crash I'll split the glass.
Behind it stands one I must kiss,
person of love or death
a person or a wraith,
I fear what I shall find.

Roy Fuller

Waiting to be Drafted

It might be any evening of spring;
The air is level, twilight in a moment
Will walk behind us and his shadow
    Fall cold across our day.

The usual trees surround an empty field
And evergreens and gravel frame the house;
Primroses lie like tickets on the ground;
    The mauve island floats on grey.

My senses are too sharp for what the mind
Presents them. In this common scene reside
Small elements with power to agitate
    And move me like a play.

I have watched a young stray dog with an affection
Of the eyes, and seen it peer from the encrusted
Lids, like a man, before it ran towards me,
    Unreasonably gay.

And watched it gnawing at a scrap of leather
In its hunger, and afterwards lying down,
Its ineffectual paws against its cracks
    Of eyes, as though to pray.

Pity and love one instant and the next
Disgust, and constantly the sense of time
Retreating, leaving events like traps: I feel
    This always, most today.

My comrades are in the house, their bodies are
At the mercy of time, their minds are nothing but yearning.
From windows where they lie, as from quiet water,
    The light is taken away.

Norman Hampson

Assault Convoy

How quietly they push the flat sea from them,
Shadows against the night, that grows to meet us
And fade back slowly to our zig-zag rhythm –
The silent pattern dim destroyers weave.
The first light greets them friendly; pasteboard ships
Erect in lineless mists of sky and sea.
A low sun lingers on the well-known outlines
That take new beauty from this sombre war-paint;
Familiar names trail childish memories
Of peace time ports and waving, gay departures.

Only at intervals the truth breaks on us
Like catspaws, ruffling these quiet waters.
Our future is unreal, a thing to read of
Later; a chapter in a history book.
We cannot see the beaches where the dead
Must fall before this waxing moon is full;
The tracer-vaulted sky, the gun's confusion,
Searchlights and shouted orders, sweaty fumbling
As landing craft are lowered; the holocaust
Grenade and bayonet will build upon these beaches.

We are dead, numbed, atrophied, sunk in the swamps of war.
Each of those thousand is a life entire.
No skilful smile can hide their sheer humanity.
Across the narrowing seas our enemies wait,
Each man the centre of his darkening world;
Bound, as we are, by humanity's traces of sorrow
To anxious women, alone in the menacing night,
Where the rhythm of Europe is lost in their private fear
And El Dorado cannot staunch their grief.

Keith Douglas

Simplify me when I'm Dead

Remember me when I am dead
and simplify me when I'm dead.

As the processes of earth
strip off the colour and the skin:
take the brown hair and blue eye

and leave me simpler than at birth,
when hairless I came howling in
as the moon entered the cold sky.

Of my skeleton perhaps,
so stripped, a learned man will say
'He was of such a type and intelligence', no more.

Thus when in a year collapse
particular memories, you may
deduce, from the long pain I bore

the opinions I held, who was my foe
and what I left, even my appearance
but incidents will be no guide.

Time's wrong-way telescope will show
a minute man ten years hence
and by distance simplified.

Through that lens see if I seem
substance or nothing; of the world
deserving mention or charitable oblivion,

not by momentary spleen
or love into decision hurled,
leisurely arrived at an opinion.

Remember me when I am dead
and simplify me when I'm dead.

Donald Bain

War Poet

We in our haste can only see the small components of the scene
We cannot tell what incidents will focus on the final screen.
A barrage of disruptive sound, a petal on a sleeping face,
Both must be noted, both must have their place;

It may be that out later selves or else our unborn sons
Will search for meaning in the dust of long deserted guns,
We only watch, and indicate and make our scribbled pencil notes.
We do not wish to moralize, only to ease our dusty throats.

Roy Campbell

Luis de Camóes

Camóes, alone, of all the lyric race,
Born in the black aurora of disaster,
Can look a common soldier in the face:
I find a comrade where I sought a master:
For daily, while the stinking crocodiles
Glide from the mangroves on the swampy shore,
He shares my awning on the dhow, he smiles,
And tells me that he lived it all before.
Through fire and shipwreck, pestilence and loss,
Led by the ignis fatuus of duty
To a dog's death – yet of his sorrows kind –
He shouldered high his voluntary Cross,
Wrestled his hardships into forms of beauty,
And taught his gorgon destinies to sing.

Keith Douglas

Desert Flowers

Living in a wide landscape are the flowers –
Rosenberg I only repeat what you were saying –
the shell and the hawk every hour
are slaying men and jerboas, slaying

the mind: but the body can fill
the hungry flowers and the dogs who cry words
at nights, the most hostile things of all.
But that is not new. Each time the night discards

draperies on the eyes and leaves the mind awake
I look each side of the door of sleep
for the little coin it will take
to buy the secret I shall not keep.

I see men as trees suffering
or confound the detail and the horizon.
Lay the coin on my tongue and I will sing
of what the others never set eyes on.

Alun Lewis

Rilke

Rilke, if you had known that I was trying
To speak to you perhaps you would have said
'Humanity has her darlings to whom she's entrusted
A farthing maybe or a jewel, at least a perception
Of what can develop and what must be always endured
And what the live may answer to the dead.
Such ones are known by their faces,
At least their absence is noted;
And they never lack an occasion,
They, the devoted.'

But I have to seek the occasion.
Labour, fatigue supervene;
The glitter of sea and land, the self-assertion
These fierce competing times insist upon.

Yet sometimes, seeking, hours glided inwards,
Laying their soft antennae on my heart,
And I forgot the thousand leagues I'd journeyed
As if Creation were about to start.

I watched the pure horizon for the earth
To rise in grey bare peaks that might enfold
The empty crumbling soil between the hands
Of coloured things a child's small fist might hold
Delightedly; I knew that unknown lands
Were near and real, like an act of birth.

Then I fell ill and restless.
Sweating and febrile all one burning week,
I hungered for the silence you acquired
And *envied* you, as though it were a gift
Presented on a birthday to the lucky.
For that which IS I thought you need not seek.

The sea is gone now and the crowded tramp
Sails other seas with other passengers.

I sit within the tent, within the darkness
Of India, and the wind disturbs my lamp.

The jackals howl and whimper in the nullah,
The goatherd sleeps upon a straw-piled bed,
And I know that in this it does not matter
Where one may be or what fate lies ahead.

And Vishnu, carved by some rude pious hand,
Lies by a heap of stones, demanding nothing
But the simplicity that she and I
Discovered in a way you'd understand
Once and for ever, Rilke, but in Oh a distant land.

Alun Lewis

To Edward Thomas   (*On visiting the memorial stone above Steep in Hampshire*)

On the way up from Sheet I met some children
Filling a pram with brushwood; higher still
Beside Steep church an old man pointed out
A rough white stone upon a flinty spur
Projecting from the high autumnal woods . . .
I doubt if much has changed since you came here
On your last leave; except the stone; it bears
Your name and trade: 'To Edward Thomas, Poet.'

II
Climbing the steep path through the copse I knew
My cares weighed heavily as yours, my gift
Much less, my hope
No more than yours.
And like you I felt sensitive and somehow apart,
Lonely and exalted by the friendship of the wind
And the placid afternoon enfolding
The dangerous future and the smile.

III
I sat and watched the dusky berried ridge
Of yew-trees, deepened by oblique dark shafts,
Throw back the flame of red and gold and russet
That leapt from beech and ash to birch and chestnut
Along the downward arc of the hill's shoulder,
And sunlight with discerning fingers
Softly explore the distant wooded acres,
Touching the farmsteads one by one with lightness
Until it reached the Downs, whose soft green pastures
Went slanting sea – and skywards to the limits
Where sight surrenders and the mind alone
Can find the sheeps' tracks and the grazing.

And for that moment Life appeared
As gentle as the view I gazed upon.

IV
Later, a whole day later, I remembered
This war and yours and your weary
Circle of failure and your striving
To make articulate the groping voices
Of snow and rain and dripping branches
And love that ailing in itself cried out
About the straggling eaves and ringed the candle
With shadows slouching round your buried head;
And in the lonely house there was no ease
For you, or Helen, or those small perplexed
Children of yours who only wished to please.

Divining this, I knew the voice that called you
Was soft and neutral as the sky
Breathing on the grey horizon, stronger
Than night's immediate grasp, the limbs of mercy
Oblivious as the blood; and growing clearer,
More urgent as all else dissolved away,
– Projected books, half-thoughts, the children's birthdays,
And wedding anniversaries as cold
As dates in history – the dream
Emerging from the fact that folds a dream,
The endless rides of stormy-branched dark
Whose fibres are a thread within the hand –

Till suddenly, at Arras, you possessed that hinted land.

Roy Fuller

War Poet

Swift had pains in his head.
Jonson dying in his bed
Tapped the dropsy himself.
Blake saw a flea and an elf.
Tennyson could hear the shriek
Of a bat. Pope was a freak.
Emily Dickinson stayed
Indoors for a decade.
Water inflated the belly
Of Hart Crane and Shelley.
Coleridge was a dope.
Southwell died on a rope.
Byron had a round white foot.
Smart and Cowper were put
Away. Lawrence was a fidget.
Keats was almost a midget.
Donne, alive in his shroud,
Shakespeare, in the coil of a cloud,
Saw death very well as he
Came crab-wise, dark and massy.
I envy not only their talents
And fertile lack of balance
But the appearance of choice
In their sad and fatal voice.

Robert Conquest

Poem in 1944

No, I cannot write the poem of war,
Neither the colossal dying nor the local scene,
A platoon asleep and dreaming of girls' warmth
Or by the petrol-cooker scraping out a laughter.
– Only the images that are not even nightmare:
A globe encrusted with a skin or seaweed,
Or razors at the roots. The heart is no man's prism
To cast a frozen shadow down the streaming future;
At most a cold slipstream of empty sorrow,
The grapes and melody of a dreamed love
Or a vague roar of courage.

     No. I am not
The meeting point of event and vision, where the poem
Bursts into flame, and the heart's engine
Takes on the load of these broken years and lifts it.
I am not even the tongue and the hand that write
The dissolving sweetness of a personal view
Like those who now in greater luck and liberty
Are professionally pitiful or heroic . . .

Into what eye to imagine the vista pouring
Its violent treasures? For I must believe
That somewhere the poet is working who can handle
The flung world and his own heart. To him I say
The little I can. I offer him the debris
Of five years undirected storm in self and Europe,
And my love. Let him take it for what it's worth
In this poem scarcely made and already forgotten.

3—Lessons of the War

Alun Lewis

All Day It has Rained . . .

All day it has rained, and we on the edge of the moors
Have sprawled in our bell-tents, moody and dull as boors,
Groundsheets and blankets spread on the muddy ground
And from the first grey wakening we have found
No refuge from the skirmishing fine rain
And the wind that made the canvas heave and flap
And the taut wet guy-ropes ravel out and snap.
All day the rain has glided, wave and mist and dream,
Drenching the gorse and heather, a gossamer stream
Too light to stir the acorns that suddenly
Snatched from their cups by the wild south-westerly
Pattered against the tent and our upturned dreaming faces.
And we stretched out, unbuttoning our braces,
Smoking a Woodbine, darning dirty socks,
Reading the Sunday papers – I saw a fox
And mentioned it in the note I scribbled home; –
And we talked of girls, and dropping bombs on Rome,
And thought of the quiet dead and the loud celebrities
Exhorting us to slaughter, and the herded refugees;
– Yet thought softly, morosely of them, and as indifferently
As of ourselves of those whom we
For years have loved, and will again
To-morrow may be love; but now it is the rain
Possesses us entirely, the twilight and the rain.

And I can remember nothing dearer or more to my heart
Than the children I watched in the woods on Saturday
Shaking down burning chestnuts for the schoolyard's merry play,
Or the shaggy patient dog who followed me
By Sheet and Steep and up the wooded scree
To the Shoulder o' Mutton where Edward Thomas brooded long
On death and beauty – till a bullet stopped his song.

Henry Reed

Lessons of the War   (*To Alan Mitchell*)

Vixi duellis nuper idoneus
Et militavi non sine gloria

1 – Naming of Parts

Today we have naming of parts. Yesterday,
We had daily cleaning. And to-morrow morning,
We shall have what to do after firing. But to-day,
To-day we have naming of parts. Japonica
Glistens like coral in all of the neighbouring gardens
   And to-day we have naming of parts.

This is the lower sling swivel. And this
Is the upper sling swivel, whose use you will see
When you are given your slings. And this is the piling swivel,
Which in your case you have not got. The branches
Hold in the gardens their silent, eloquent gestures,
   Which in our case we have not got.

This is the safety-catch, which is always released
With an easy flick of the thumb. And please do not let me
See anyone using his finger. You can do it quite easy
If you have any strength in your thumb. The blossoms
Are fragile and motionless, never letting anyone see
   Any of them using their finger.

And this you can see is the bolt. The purpose of this
Is to open the breech, as you see. We can slide it
Rapidly backwards and forwards; we call this
Easing the spring. And rapidly backwards and forwards
The early bees are assaulting and fumbling the flowers:
   They call it easing the Spring.

They call it easing the Spring; it is perfectly easy
If you have any strength in your thumb; like the bolt,
And the breech, and the cocking-piece, and the point of balance,
Which in our case we have not got; and the almond-blossom

Silent in all of the gardens and the bees going backwards and
    forwards,
      For today we have naming of parts.

II – Judging Distances

Not only how far away, but the way that you say it
Is very important. Perhaps you may never get
The knack of judging a distance, but at least you know
How to report on a landscape; the central sector,
The right of arc and that, which we had last Tuesday,
      And at least you know

That maps are of time, not place, as far as the army
Happens to be concerned – the reason being,
Is one which need not delay us. Again, you know
There are three kinds of tree, three only, the fir and the poplar,
And those which have bushy tops to; and lastly
      That things only seem to be things.

A barn is not called a barn, to put it more plainly,
Or a field in the distance, where sheep may be safely grazing.
You must never be over-sure. You must say, when reporting:
At five o'clock in the central sector is a dozen
Of what appear to be animals; whatever you do,
      Don't call the bleeders *sheep*.

I am sure that's quite clear; and suppose, for the sake of example,
The one at the end, asleep, endeavours to tell us
What he sees over there to the west, and how far away,
After first having come to attention. There to the west
On the fields of summer the sun and the shadows bestow
      Vestments of purple and gold.

The still white dwellings are like a mirage in the heat,
And under the swaying elms a man and a woman
Lie gently together. Which is, perhaps, only to say

That there is a row of houses to the left of arc,
And that under some poplars a pair of what appear to be humans
 Appear to be loving.

Well, that for an answer, is what we might rightly call
Moderately satisfactory only, the reason being,
Is that two things have been omitted, and those are important.
The human beings, now: in what direction are they,
And how far away, would you say? And do not forget
 There may be dead ground in between.

There may be dead ground in between; and I may not have got
The knack of judging a distance; I will only venture
A guess that perhaps between me and the apparent lovers,
(Who, incidentally, appear by now to have finished,)
At seven o'clock from the houses, is roughly a distance
 Of about one year and a half.

III – Unarmed Combat

In due course of course you will all be issued with
Your proper issue; but until tomorrow,
You can hardly be said to need it; and until that time,
We shall have unarmed combat. I shall teach you.
The various holds and rolls and throws and breakfalls
 Which you may sometimes meet.

And the various holds and rolls and throws and breakfalls
Do not depend on any sort of weapon,
But only on what I might coin a phrase and call
The ever-important question of human balance,
And the ever-important need to be in a strong
 Position at the start.

There are many kinds of weakness about the body,
Where you would least expect, like the ball of the foot.
But the various holds and rolls and throws and breakfalls

Will always come in useful. And never be frightened
To tackle from behind; it may not be clean to do so,
    But this is global war.

So give them all you have, and always give them
As good as you get; it will always get you somewhere.
(You may not know it, but you can tie a Jerry
Up without rope; it is one of the things I shall teach you.)
Nothing will matter if only you are ready for him.
    The readiness is all.

The readiness is all. How can I help but feel
I have been here before? But somehow then,
I was the tied-up one. How to get out
Was always then my problem. And even if I had
A piece of rope I was always the sort of person
    Who threw the rope aside.

And in my time I have given them all I had,
Which was never as good as I got, and it got me nowhere.
And the various holds and rolls and throws and breakfalls
Somehow or other I always seemed to put
In the wrong place. And as for war, my wars
    Were global from the start.

Perhaps I was never in a strong position,
Or the ball of my foot got hurt, or I had some weakness
Where I had least expected. But I think I see your point.
While awaiting a proper issue, we must learn the lesson
Of the ever-important question of human balance.
    It is courage that counts.

Things may be the same again; and we must fight
Not in the hope of winning but rather of keeping
Something alive: so that when we meet our end,
It may be said that we tackled wherever we could,
That battle-fit we lived, and though defeated,
    Not without glory fought.

Alun Lewis

The Public Gardens

Only a few top-heavy hollyhocks, wilting in arid beds,
Frayed lawns,
Twin sycamores storing the darkness massively under balconies of
    leaf,
And an empty rococo bandstand – strangely unpopular
Saturday evening in the public gardens.

But wait: These take their places:

A thin little woman in black stockings and a straw hat with wax
    flowers,
Holding a varnished cane with both hands against her spent knees
As she sits alone on the bench, yes oddly
Alone and at rest:

An older wealthier lady, gesticulating and over-dressed,
Puffily reciting the liturgy of vexations
To her beautiful companion,
The remote and attractive demi-Parnassian
Whose dark hair catches the sunlight as she listens
With averted face and apparent understanding:

A boy with his crutches laid against the wall
Pale in the shadow where the hops hang over
In light green bundles; – is he, too, waiting
For one who perhaps
Prefers another?
And I, forgetting my khaki, my crude trade,
And the longing that has vexed and silenced me all the day,
Now simply consider the quiet people,
How their pattern emerges as the evening kindles
Till the park is a maze of diagonal, ah far
Too fine to catch the sun like the glittering webs
The spiders have folded and flung from the fading privet.

Only the children, passionately,
Snap my drifting lines with laughter
As they chase each other among the benches
In and out of the dreaming gardens.

Roy Fuller

The Petty Officers' Mess

Just now I wished the monkeys; they
Are captive near the mess. And so the day
Ends simply with a sudden darkness, while
Again across the palm trees, like a file,
    The rain swings from the bay.

The radio speaks, the light attract the flies,
Above them and the rain our voices rise,
And somewhere from this hot and trivial place
As the news tells of death, with pleasant face,
    Comes that which is not lies.

The voices argue: *Soldiers in the end*
Turn scarecrows; their ambiguous figures blend
With all who are obsessed by food and peace.
The rulers go, they cannot order these
    Who are not disciplined.

O cars with abdicating princes: streets
Of untidy crowds: O terrible defeats!
Such images which haunt us of the past
Flash on the present like the exile's vast
    Shivers and fleshy heats;

But never coincide. Do they approach?
Upon that doubt I'm frightened to encroach –
Show me, I say, *the organizations that*
Will charge the rags and mob into the state
    Like pumpkin into coach.

The voices make no answer. Music now
Throbs through the room and I remember how
The little pickaxe shapes of swallows swerve
From balconies and whitewashed walls; a curve
    Of bird-blue bay; a dhow;

Small stabbing observations! And I know
(The cheap song says it on the radio)
That nerves and skin first suffer when we part,
The deep insensitive tissues of the heart
    Later, when time is slow.

And time has down his part and stands and looks
With dumb exasperated face. The books
Year after year record the crisis and
The passion, but no change. The measuring sand
    Is still, There are no flukes,

Like the virtuous sulphonamides, to kill
The poisons of the age, but only will:
Reduction of desires to that cold plan
Of raping the ideal; the new frail man
    Who slays what's in the hill.

The monkeys near the mess (where we all eat
And dream) I saw tonight select with neat
And brittle fingers dirty scraps, and fight,
And then look pensive in the fading light,
    And after pick their feet.

They are secured by straps about their slender
Waists, and the straps to chains. Most sad and tender,
They clasp each other and look around with eyes
Like ours at what their strange captivities
    Invisibly engender.

Gavin Ewart

Officers' Mess

It's going to be a thick night tonight (and the night before was a
   thick one),
I've just seen the Padre disappearing into 'The Cock' for a quick
   one.
I don't mind telling you this, old boy, we got the Major drinking –
You probably know the amount of gin he's in the habit of sinking–
And then that new MO came in, the Jewish one, awful fellow,
And his wife, a nice little bit of stuff, dressed in a flaming yellow.
Looked a pretty warmish piece, old boy, – no, have this one with
   me –
They were both so blind (and so was the Major) that they could
   hardly see.
She had one of those amazing hats and a kind of silver fox fur
(I wouldn't mind betting several fellows have had a go at her).
She made a bee-line for the Major, bloody funny, old boy,
Asked him a lot about horses and India, you know, terribly coy –
And this MO fellow was mopping it up and at last he passed right
   out
(Some silly fool behind his back put a bottle of gin in his stout).
I've never seen a man go down so quick. Somebody drove him
   home.
His wife was almost as bad, old boy, said she felt all alone
And nestled up to the Major – it's a great pity you weren't there –
And the Padre was arguing about the order of morning and
   evening prayer.
Never laughed so much in all my life. We went on drinking till
   three.
And this bloody woman was doing her best to sit on the Major's
   knee!
Let's have the blackout boards put up and turn on the other light.
Yes, I think you can count on that, old boy – tonight'll be a thick
   night.

Alan Ross

Mess Deck

The bulkhead sweating, and under naked bulbs
Men writing letters, playing Ludo. The light
Cuts their arms off at the wrist, only the dice
Lives. Hammocks swing, nuzzling-in tight
Like foals into flanks of mares. Bare shoulders
Glisten with oil, tattoo-marks rippling their scales on
Mermaids or girls' thighs as dice are shaken, cards played.
We reach for sleep like a gas, randy for oblivion.
But, laid out on lockers, some get waylaid;
And lie stiff, running off films in the mind's dark-room.
The air soupy, yet still cold; a beam sea rattles
Cups smelling of stale tea, knocks over a broom.
The light is watery, like the light of the sea-bed;
Marooned in it, stealthy as fishes, we may even be dead.

Charles Causley

Chief Petty Officer

He is older than the naval side of British history,
And sits
More permanent than the spider in the enormous wall.
His barefoot, coal-burning soul,
Expands, puffs like a toad, in the convict air
Of the Royal Naval Barracks at Devonport.

Here in depot, is his stone Nirvana:
More real than the opium pipes,
The uninteresting relics of Edwardian foreign-commission.
And, from his thick stone box,
He surveys with a prehistoric eye the hostilities-only ratings.
He has the face of the dinosaur
That sometimes stares from old Victorian naval photographs:
That of some elderly lieutenant
With boots and a celluloid Crippen-collar,
Brass buttons and cruel ambitious eyes of almond.

He was probably made a Freemason in Hong Kong.
He has a son (on War Work) in the Dockyard,
and an appalling daughter
In the WRNS
He writes on your draft-chit,
Tobacco-permit or request-form
In a huge antique Borstal hand,
And pins notices on the board in the Chiefs' Mess
Requesting his messmates not to
Lay on the billard table.
He is an anti-Semite, and has somewhat reactionary views,
And reads the pictures in the daily news.

And when you return from the nervous Pacific
Where the seas
Shift like sheets of plate-glass in the dazzling morning;
Or when you return
Browner than Alexander, from Malta,
Where you have leaned over the side, in harbour,

And seen in the clear water
The salmon-tins, wrecks and tiny explosions of crystal fish,
A whole war later
He will still be sitting under a purser's clock
Waiting for tot-time,
His narrow forehead ruffled by the Jutland wind.

Norman Cameron

Punishment Enough

They say that women, in a bombing-raid,
Retire to sleep in brand-new underwear
Lest they be tumbled out of doors, displayed
In shabby garments to the public stare.

You've often seen a house, sliced like a cheese,
Displaying its poor secrets – peeling walls
And warping cupboards. Of such tragedies
It is the petty scale that most appals.

When you confess your sins before a parson,
You find it no great effort to disclose
Your crimes of murder, bigamy and arson,
But can you tell him that you pick your nose?

If after death you pay for your misdeeds,
Surely the direst and most just requital
Would be to listen while an angel reads
Before a crowd your endless, mean recital:

Golf scorecards faked, thefts from your mother's purse ...
But why should Doomsday bother with such stuff?
This is the Hell that you already nurse
Within you. You've had punishment enough.

Herbert Corby

Reprisal

They worked all night with cardboard and with wood
to make those dummy planes to hoodwink the foe,
and in the chilly morning solitude
wheeled out the dummies to places they should go
on the dispersal fields, and went away;
the hours passed uneventfully, and even
no reconnaissance planes were overhead that day.
They evacuated in the twilight, just after seven,
and when they'd gone the Germans flew above the drome
and by each plane they dropped a wooden bomb.

Norman Cameron

Black Takes White

On the Italian front there was a sector
That neither side had any great respect for.
Jerry looked down from a west-Appenine hill-mass
That one brigade could hold from now to Christmas,
While, for attack, he had no troops to squander.
In fact, the show was largely propaganda:
The Yanks had negroes, Jerry had Italians,
In regular divisions and battalions
To prove that they were pukka fighting allies;
Though plainly neither mob had an relish
For warfare (and why should they, lacrima Christi!
Negroes for Jays, peasants for squadristi?)
The only major movement in those quarters
Was a dense, two-way traffic of deserters.

It chanced that a deserting negro party
Encountered a like-minded Eytie.
At this a keen discussion was engendered,
Each party claiming that it had surrendered
And that the other had become its captor.
The Eyties held the trump, the winning factor:
Their lot was led by an ufficiale;
What *he* said, went. (The tale's a tribute, really,
To both sides' rather narrow sense of duty.)
Back marched the negroes with their unsought booty.

Imagine how the PRO's got cracking!
Here was the feat of arms they'd long been lacking.
Nobody paused to bother with such trifles
As where the captors had mislaid their rifles.
Quickly those fed-up and embarrassed negroes
Were praised, promoted, given gongs as heroes,
And photographs of their victorious battle
Were published from Long Island to Seattle.

R. N. Currey

Disintegration of Springtime

This is a damned unnatural sort of war;
The pilot sits among the clouds, quite sure
About the values he is fighting for;
He cannot hear beyond his veil of sound,

He cannot see the people on the ground;
He only knows that on the sloping map
Of sea-fringed town and country people creep
Like ants – and who cares if ants laugh or weep?

To us he is no more than a machine
Shown on an instrument; what can he mean
In human terms? – a man, somebody's son,
Proud of his skill; compact of flesh and bone
Fragile as Icarus – and our desire
To see that damned machine come down on fire.

Alan Ross

Off Brighton Pier

I saw him, a squat man with red hair,
Grown into sideburns, fishing off Brighton pier;
Suddenly he bent, and in a lumpy bag
Rummaged for bait, letting his line dangle,
And I noticed the stiffness of his leg
That thrust out, like a tripod, at an angle.
Then I remembered: the sideburns, that gloss
Of slicked-down ginger on a skin like candy floss
He was there, not having moved, as last,
On a windless night, leaning against the mast,
I saw him, groping a bag for numbers.
And the date was the 17th of September,
15 years back, and we were playing Tombola
During the last Dog, someone beginning to holler
'Here you are' for a full card, and I remember
He'd just called 'Seven and six, she was worth it,'
When – without contact or warning – we were hit.
Some got away with it, a few bought it.
And I recall now, when they carried him ashore,
Fishing gear lashed to his hammock, wishing
Him luck, and his faint smile, more
To himself than to me, when he saluted
From the stretcher, and, cadging a fag,
Cracked 'I'm quids in, it's only one leg,
They'll pension me off to go fishing.'

4—'Goodbye for a Long Time'

Roy Fuller

Goodbye for a Long Time

The furnished room beyond the stinging of
The sea, reached by a gravel road in which
Puddles of rain stare up with clouded eyes:

The photographs of other lives than ours;
The scattered evidence of your so brief
Possession; daffodils fading in a vase.

Our kisses have as they have always been,
Half sensual, half scared, bringing like
A scent our years together, crowds of ghosts.

And then among the thousand thoughts of parting
The kisses grow perfunctory; the years
Are waved away by your retreating arm.

And now I am alone. I am once more
The far-off boy without a memory,
Wandering with an empty deadened self.

Suddenly under my feet there is the small
Body of a bird, startling against the gravel.
I see its tight shut eye, a trace of moisture.

And ruffling its gentle breast the wind, its beak
Sharpened by death; and I am yours again,
Hurt beyond hurting, never to forget.

Alun Lewis

Goodbye

So we must say Goodbye, my darling,
And go, as lovers go, for ever;
Tonight remains, to pack and fix on labels
And make an end of lying down together.

I put a final shilling in the gas,
And watch you slip your dress below your knees
And lie so still I hear your rustling comb
Modulate the autumn in the trees.

And all the countless things I shall remember
Lay mummy-cloths of silence round my head;
I fill the carafe with a drink of water;
You say 'We paid a guinea for this bed,'

And then, 'We'll leave some gas, a little warmth
For the next resident, and those dry flowers,'
And turn your face away, afraid to speak
The big wood, that Eternity is ours.

Your kisses close my eyes and yet you stare
As though God struck a child with nameless fears;
Perhaps the water glitters and discloses
Time's chalice and its limpid useless tears.

Everything we renounce except ourselves;
Selfishness is the last of all to go;
Our sighs are exhalations of the earth,
Our footprints leave a track across the snow.

We made the universe to be our home,
Our nostrils took the wind to be our breath,
Our hearts are massive towers of delight,
We stride across the seven seas of death.

Yet when all's done you'll keep the emerald
I placed upon your finger in the street;
And I will keep the patches that you sewed
On my old battle-dress tonight, my sweet.

Keith Douglas

The Prisoner

To-day, Cheng, I touched your face
with two fingers, as a gesture of love;
for I can never prove enough
by sight or sense your strange grace,

but mothwise my hands return
to your fair cheek, as luminous
as a lamp in a paper house,
and touch, to teach love and learn.

I think a hundred hours are gone
that so, like gods, we'd occupy.
But alas, Cheng, I cannot tell why,
today I touched a mask stretched on the stone

person of death. There was the urge
to break the bright flesh and emerge
of the ambitious cruel bone.

Drummond Allison

Leave Poem

So you may cross the Corn and run uncaring
To tea at Merton; while the steps of Queen's
Hold from the High Street still and still seem fearing
To encroach upon it, but the city leans
Towards you which would never let me touch
(Though each strong stone had desperate patience then to teach).

You need not bother now to leave the note
Or know about the book, not now suspect
The self-propelled surprise the weekly wait;
For I've set up my soviet to elect
My own new rulers now, and only Death
Can quash this constitution and subject us both.

His is the only bed we'll ever share
And ours the love of different soil on soil
– Yes, there's one date I never need prepare
Against your breaking, darling. But meanwhile
Lie on the lesbian river and delude
Whatever pausing oarsman thinks he is obeyed.

And I'll make eastward haste for eager Dover,
The waving friends and flags, the naval types
In permanent pressgangs with their slopping bitter:
Those friends confer, that wary barmaid wipes,
Till I've no time to visit you but over
Go to my faithful flocks of swans in long Larne harbour.

Julian Symons

Eleven Meetings

Between nothing and their first meeting
Was the paraphernalia of greeting,
Hand touching on hand, the sudden
Look from which nothing is hidden.

Between their first and tenth meeting
Was a short time but much loving,
The days long and the nights longer,
Till Death spoke with gun in his anger.

Between their tenth and last meeting
Was nothing; but at last the weeping
Face with which she regarded sadly
His face looking up at her coldly.

H. B. Mallalieu

Platform Goodbye

My hand waving from the window
Felt still the touch of your fingers:
Sorrow that made me dumb
Becomes pride in your love: and now,
As you turn the key in the door,
Or enter the room where our lives
Are still touched by the cushions and cards,
The tea gone cold in the cups,
My train takes me as though through sleep
To an empty room and the night.

I cannot delude my sense. The cards
Through my fingers slip. Loneliness
Brings you near, a tear's reach from my hand:
But from the flower at your neck
The colours already fade.

It is not these tangible things
That give me strength to endure,
But the echo still of you voice
In the deep abyss of my heart:
The way you stare through my eyes,
The intimate touch of your hand
On this pencil with which I write;

The years we have shared will give
To the hive of our senses both,
Honey to sharpen the taste
Of the years while our bodies lie
Lonely and separately.

The hammering in my heart
Forges from sorrow pride
As the train draws us apart.

Though the hurt under the flesh
Spreads like the numbness of snow,
My love is in all you do,
Yours with me wherever I go.

Alan Ross

Leave Train

Yellow as flowers as dead fingers
Yellow as death as a mandarin
Dawn with eyes like a stranger
Dawn with a handful of sick flowers.

The stumps of memory are broken trees
The stumps of memory are amputated fingers
The patient sick with ether
Dreams unflowered avenues of anger.

Grief clenched like a fist, a
Sprawled hand, grief pitted with shell.
The bell of the blood in a deep sea
Drowns, the hood of the face is eyeless.

Dawn constellated with sick stars
Dawn hedged round with smoke
Yellow as fog as cornflowers
Yellow as a dog as a death's head.

Like dissevered arteries and veins
Like brain cauterized and eyes
Protuberant with grief, the staring
Unbelief writhes bloodshot

In the tearless lids. The massed weirs,
Frozen of feeling, are empty with disuse.
Without you without you without you
Branches like nerves are sporadic with fever.

Yellow as dead flowers as a remembered South
Yellow as desire as face to face
Dawn with a handful of unnecessary hours
Dawn with cut flowers and a mouth of disaster.

Alun Lewis

Dawn on the East Coast

From Orford Ness to Shingle Street
The grey disturbance spreads
Washing the icy seas on Deben Head.

Cock pheasants scratch the frozen fields,
Gulls lift thin horny legs and step
Fastidiously among the rusted mines.

The soldier leaning on the sandbagged wall
Hears in the combers' curling rush and crash
His single, self-centred monotonous wish;

And time is a froth of such transparency
His drowning eyes see what they wish to see;
A girl laying his table with a white cloth.

....

The light assails him from a flank,
Two carbons touching in his brain
Crumple the cellophane lanterns of his dream.

And then the day, grown feminine and kind,
Stoops with the gulfing motion of the tide
And pours his ashes in a tiny urn.

From Orford Ness to Shingle Street
The grey disturbance lifts its head
And one by one, reluctantly,
The living come back slowly from the dead.

Alun Lewis

Sacco Writes to his Son

I did not want to die. I wanted you,
You and your sister Inez and your mother.
Reject this death, my Dante, seek out Life,
Yet not the death-in-life that most men live.
My body aches . . . I think I hear you weep.
You must not weep. Tears are a waste of strength.
Seven years your mother wept, not as your mother,
But as my wife. So make her more your mother.
Take her the ways I know she can escape
From the poor soulness that so wearies her.
Take her into the country every Sunday,
Ask her the name of such and such a plant,
Gather a basket each of herbs and flowers,
Ask her to find the robin where he nests,
She will be happy then. Tears do no damage
That spring from gladness, though they scald the throat.
Go patiently about it. Not too much
Just yet, Dante, good boy. You'll know.

And for yourself, remember in the play
Of happiness you must not act alone.
The joy is in the sharing of the feast.
Also be like a man in how you greet
The suffering that makes your young face thin.
Be not perturbed if you are called to fight.
Only a fool thinks life was made his way,
A fool or the daughter of a wealthy house.
Husband yourself, but never stale your mind
with prudence or with doubting. I could wish
You saw my body slipping from the chair
Tomorrow. You'd remember that, my son,
And would not weigh the cost of our struggle
Against the product as a poor wife does.
But I'll not break your sleep with such a nightmare.

You looked so happy when you lay asleep . . .

But I have neither strength nor room for all
these thoughts. One single thought's enough
To fill immensity. I drop my pen . . .

I hope this letter finds you in good health,
My son, my comrade. Will you give my love
To Inez and your mother and my friends.
Bartolo also sends his greetings to you.
I would have written better and more simple
Except my head spins like a dancing top
And my hand trembles . . . I am Oh, so weak, . . .

Alun Lewis

Postscript: For Gweno

If I should go away,
Beloved, do not say
'He has forgotten me'.
For you abide,
A singing rib within my dreaming side;
You always stay.
And in the mad tormented valley
Where blood and hunger rally
And Death the wild beast is uncaught, untamed,
Our soul withstands the terror
And has its quiet honour
Among the glittering stars your voices named.

5—A Traveller's Eye

Bernard Gutteridge

Shillong

I crowd all earth into a traveller's eye
Fragment by fragment. Only he
Can see the withering scar or sublime flower
For the first time joined in his own hour.

The market strewn with gutted fish; and fruit
Spewed open for the kites; the cries
And foul and sultry smell. A revered priest
Stooping in ashes: the greatest, the least.

Testing North towards Tibet the cold
Austere horizon of coarse green pines
Holds trapped the waterfall. The wide sky throws
White clouds towards the annihilating snows.

Bernard Gutteridge

Bombay

In Hornby Road and the Yacht Club, Bombay
Shines on as brightly as a playing card
Where still the Europeans boss and play:
Kings and Queens slightly part-worn, fit to discard.

Pavements are stippled with people. Jacks
Have fun as in Brighton shiny with bounders.
The Taj gives them its icy gins, almonds and snacks.
Along the grey edge of the sea the harbour flounders.

A dead forest of masts flowering in shifting gulls.
Slow sails on the water, tall sea lilies fawn,
The cricket ground tries to defeat the ocean and lulls
With pink and white deck chairs and strawberries on the green lawn.

Like any great city until the web of noises waves
About you and holds you. The threatening noises in the street:
That dissonant horny quack of dry leaves;
And shuffle of bare feet on burning concrete.

The spying rustle of noise the white clothes –
Saris and dhotis – shake across a room.
Head turning hiss and grunt of a man who loathes
Our race and shows it. Drums in the small temples like doom

All night, as, bound Eastwards for the war,
The open casual West a memory growing less,
We move into the dark and sense once more
This sinister city uncoil its venomed softness.

Alun Lewis

Port of Call: Brazil

We watch the heavy-odoured beast
Of darkness crouch along the water-front
Under the town exorcised by the priest.
The lights entice the paramours to hunt.

Tropical thunder creams the glassy bay,
White sails on bamboo masts disturb the night,
The troopship turns and drags upon her stay,
The portholes cast a soft, subjective light.

And we who crowd in hundreds to the side
Feel the lights prick us with a grey distaste
As though we had some guilty thing to hide –
We, who thought the negroes were debased

This morning when they scrambled on the quay
For what we threw, and from their dugout boats
Haggled cigars and melons raucously
Lifting their bleating faces like old goats.

But now the white-faced tourist must translate
His old unsated longing to adventure
Beyond the European's measured hate
Into the dangerous oceans of past and future

Where trembling intimations will reveal
The illusion of this blue mulatto sleep
And in that chaos like a migrant eel
Will breed a new direction through the deep.

Alun Lewis

The Mahratta Ghats

The valleys crack and burn, the exhausted plains
Sink their black teeth into the horny veins
Straggling the hills' red thighs, the bleating goats
– Dry bents and bitter thistles in their throats –
Thread the loose rocks by immemorial tracks.
Dark peasants drag the sun upon their backs.

High on the ghat the new turned soil is red,
The sun has ground it to the finest red,
It lies like gold within each horny hand.
Siva has spilt his seed upon this land.

Will she who burns and withers on the plain
Leave, ere too late, her scraggy herds of pain,
The cow-dung fire and the trembling beasts,
The little wicked gods, the grinning priests,
And climb, before a thousand years have fled,
High as the eagle to her mountain bed
Whose soil is fine as flour and blood-red?

But no! She cannot move. Each arid patch
Owns the lean folk who plough and scythe and thatch
Its grudging yield and scratch its stubborn stones.
The small gods suck the marrow from their bones.

Who is it climbs the summit of the road?
Only the beggar bumming his dark load.
Who was it cried to see the falling star?
Only the landless soldier lost in war.

And did a thousand years go by in vain?
And does another thousand start again?

Alun Lewis

The Jungle

In mole-blue indolence the sun
Plays idly on the stagnant pool
In whose grey bed black swollen leaf
Holds Autumn rotting like an unfrocked priest.
The crocodiles slides from the ochre sand
And drives the great translucent fish
Under the boughs across the running gravel.
Windfalls of brittle mast crunch as we come
To quench more than our thirst – our selves –
Beneath this bamboo bridge, this mantled pool
Where sleep exudes a sinister content
As though all strength of mind and limb must pass
And all fidelities and doubts dissolve,
The weighted world a bubble in each head,
The warm pacts of the flesh betrayed
By the nonchalance of a laugh,
The green indifference of this sleep.

II

Wandering and fortuitous the paths
We followed to this rendezvous today
Out of the mines and offices and dives,
The sidestreets of anxiety and want,
Huge cities known and distant as the stars,
Wheeling beyond our destiny and hope.
We did not notice how the accent changed
As shadows ride from precipice to plain
Closing the parks and cordoning the roads,
Clouding the humming cultures of the West –
The weekly bribe we paid the man in black,

The day shift sinking from the sun,
The blinding arc of rivets blown through steel,
The patient queues, headlines and slogans flung
Across a frightened continent, the town
Sullen and out of work, the little home

Semi-detached, suburban, transient
As fever or the anger of the old,
The best ones on some specious pretext gone

But we who dream beside this jungle pool
Prefer the instinctive rightness of the poised
Pied kingfisher deep darting for a fish
To all the banal rectitudes of states,
The dew-bright diamonds on a viper's back
To the slow poison of a meaning lost
And the vituperations of the just.

III

The banyan's branching clerestories close
The noon's harsh splendour to a head of light.
The black spot in the focus grows and grows:
The vagueness of the child, the lover's deep
And inarticulate bewilderment,
The willingness to please that made a wound,
The kneeling darkness and the hungry prayer;
Cargoes of anguish in the holds of joy,
The smooth deceitful stranger in the heart,
The tangled wrack of motives drifting down
An oceanic tide of Wrong.
And though the state has enemies we know
The greater enmity within ourselves.

Some things we cleaned like knives in earth,
Kept from the dew and rust of Time
Instinctive truths and elemental love,
Knowing the force that brings the teal and quail
From Turkestan across the Himalayan snows
To Kashmir and the South alone can guide
That winging wildness home again.

Oh you who want us for ourselves,
Whose love can start a snow-rush in the woods
And melt the glacier in the dark coulisse,
Forgive this strange inconstancy of soul,
The face distorted in a jungle pool
That drowns its image in a mort of leaves.

IV

Grey monkeys jibber, ignorant and wise.
We are the ghosts, and they the denizens;
We are like them anonymous, unknown,
Avoiding what is human, near,
Skirting the villages, the paddy fields
Where boys sit timelessly to scare the crows
On bamboo platforms raised above their lives.

A trackless wilderness divides
Joy from its cause, the motive from the act:
The killing arm uncurls, strokes the soft moss;
The distant world is an obituary,
We do not hear the tappings of its dread.
The act sustains; there is no consequence.
Only aloneness, swinging slowly
Down the cold orbit of an older world
Than any they predicted in the schools,
Stirs the cold forest with a starry wind,
And sudden as the flashing of a sword
The dream exalts the bowed and golden head
And time is swept with a great turbulence,
The old temptation to remould the world.

The bamboos creak like an uneasy house;
The night is shrill with crickets, cold with space.
And if the mute pads on the sand should lift
Annihilating paws and strike us down

Then would some unimportant death resound
With the imprisoned music of the soul?
And we become the world we could not change?
Or does the will's long struggle end
With the last kindness of a foe or friend?

Norman Cameron

Green, Green is El Aghir

Sprawled on the crates and sacks in the rear of the truck,
I was gummy-mouthed from the sun and the dust of the track,
And the two Arab soldiers I'd taken on as hitch-hikers
At a torrid petrol-dump, had been there on their hunkers
Since early morning. I said, in a kind of French
'On m'a dit, qu'il y a une belle source d'eau fraîche,
Plus loin, à El Aghir' . . .

        It was eighty more kilometres
Until round a corner we heard a splashing of waters,
And there, in a green, dark street, was a fountain with two faces
Discharging both ways, from full-throated faucets
Into basins, thence into troughs and thence into brooks.
Our negro corporal driver slammed his brakes,
And we yelped and leapt from the truck and went at the double
To fill our bidons and bottles and drink and dabble.
Then, swollen with water, we went to an inn for wine.
The Arabs came, too, though their faith might have stood between.
'After all,' they said, 'it's a boisson', without contrition.

Green, green is El Aghir. It has a railway-station,
And the wealth of its soil has born many another fruit,
A mairie, a school and an elegant Salle de Fêtes.
Such blessings, as I remarked, in effect, to the waiter,
Are added unto them that have plenty of water.

Keith Douglas

Egypt

Aniseed has a sinful taste:
at your elbow a woman's voice
like, I imagine, the voice of ghosts,
demanding food. She has no grace

but, diseased and blind of an eye
and heavy with habitual dolour,
listlessly finds you and I
and the table are the same colour.

The music, the harsh talk, the fine
clash of the drinkseller's tray,
are the same to her, as her own whine;
she knows no variety.

And in fifteen years of living
found nothing different from death
but the difference of moving
the nuisance of breath.

A disguise of ordure can't hide
her beauty, succumbing in a cloud
of disease, disease, apathy. My God,
the king of this country must be proud.

Keith Douglas

Syria

The grasses, ancient enemies
waiting at the edge of towns
conceal a movement of live stones,
the lizards with hooded eyes
of hostile miraculous age.

It is not snow on the green space
of hilltops, only towns of white
whose trees are populous with fruit
and girls whose velvet beauty is
handed down to them, gentle ornaments.

Here I am a stranger clothed
in the separative glass cloak
of strangeness. The dark eyes, the bright-mouthed
smiles, glance on the glass and break
falling like fine strange insects.

But from the grass, the inexorable lizard,
the dart of hatred for all strangers finds
in this armour, proof only against friends
breach after breach, and like the gnat is busy
wounding the skin, leaving poison there.

Jocelyn Brooke

Landscape Near Tobruk

This land was made for War. As glass
Resists the bite of vitriol, so this hard
And calcined earth rejects
The battle's hot, corrosive impact. Here
Is no nubile, girlish land, no green
And virginal countryside for War
To violate. This land is hard,
Inviolable; the battle's aftermath
Presents no ravaged and emotive scene,
No landscape à la Goya. Here are no trees
Uprooted, gutted farms; the unsalvaged scrap –
The scattered petrol-cans, the upturned
And abandoned truck, the fallen Heinkel; all
The rusted and angular detritus
Of war, seem scarcely to impinge
Upon the hard, resistant surface of
This lunar land: ephemeral
As trippers' leavings, paper-bags and orange-peel
Upon Ben Nevis. Sun and sand
Inhibit here the mind's habitual
And easy gestures; hand and eye
Perform their functions with a robot-cunning –
The sly and casual movements of
The shadowed thief. The soldiers camped
In the rock-strewn wadi merge
Like lizard or jerboa in the brown
And neutral ambient: stripped at gunsite,
Or splashing like glad beasts at sundown in
The brackish pool, their smooth
And lion-coloured bodies seem
The indigenous fauna of an unexplored,
Unspoiled country: harmless, easy to trap,
And tender-fleshed – a hunter's prize.

Roy Fuller

In Africa

Parabolas of grief, the hills are never
Hills and the plains,
Where through the torrid air the lions shiver,
No longer plains.

Just as the lives of lions now are made
Shabby with rifles,
This great geography shrinks into sad
And personal trifles.

For those who are in love and are exiled
Can never discover
How to be happy: looking upon the wild
They see for ever

The cultivated acre of their pain;
The clouds like dreams,
Involved, improbable; the endless plain
Precisely as it seems.

Roy Fuller

The Giraffes

I think before they saw me the giraffes
Were watching me. Over the golden grass,
The bush and ragged open tree of thorn,
From a grotesque height, under their lightish horns,
Their eyes were fixed on mine as I approached them.
The hills behind descended steeply; iron-
Coloured outcroppings of rock half-covered by
Dull green and sepia vegetation, dry
And sunlit; and above, the piercing blue
Where clouds like islands lay or like swans flew.

Seen from those hills the scrubby plain is like
A large-scale map whose features have a look
Half-menacing, half familiar, and across
Its brightness arms of shadow ceaselessly
Revolve. Like small forked twigs or insects move
Giraffes, upon the great map where they live.

When I went nearer, their long bovine tails
Flicked loosely, and deliberately they turned,
An undulation of dappled grey and brown,
And stood in profile with those curious planes
Of neck and sloping haunches. Just as when,
Quite motionless, they watched I never thought
Them moved by fear, a wish to be a tree,
So as they put more ground between us!
Saw evidence that these were animals
With no desire for intercourse, or no
Capacity.
                          Above the falling sun,
Like visible winds the clouds are streaked and spun,
And cold and dark now bring the image of
Those creatures walking without pain or love.

Roy Campbell

Snapshot of Nairobi

With orange-peel the streets are strown
And pips, beyond computing,
On every shoulder but my own,
That's fractured with saluting.

Henry Reed

Sailors' Harbour

My thoughts, like sailors becalmed in Cape Town harbour,
Await your return, like a favourable wind, or like
New tackle for the voyage, without which it is useless starting.
We watch the sea daily, finish our daily tasks
By ten in the morning, and with the day to waste,
Wander through the suburbs, with quiet thoughts of the brothels,
And sometimes thoughts of the churches.

In the eating houses we always contrive to get near to
The window, where we can keep an eye on the life-
Bearing sea. Suddenly a wind might blow, and we must not miss
First sight of the waves as they darken with promise for us.
We have been here too long. We know the quays,
And the streets near the quays, more than should ever be necessary.
When can we go on our way?

Certain we are of this, that when the wind comes,
It may be deceptive and sweet and finally blow
To shipwreck and ruin between here and the next port of call.
At all times we think of this. At last we have come to know
The marine charts can safely assure us of less and less
As we go farther south. So we cannot go out of the boulevards
Or climb Table Mountain,

Though if we had certainty, here there might be delight.
But all that is world in itself, the mountain, the streets,
The sand-dunes outside the town, we shyly and sadly return from.
They are too much to bear. And our curiosity
Lies alone in the over-scrubbed decks and the polished brasses
(For we have to look trim in the port) and in
The high-piled ambiguous cargo.

Alan Ross

Iceland in Wartime

Green and red lights flank the inlet mouth,
As it were a night-club. But three days south,
Below grey Scottish hills, I read a book
About this island, arranged mentally its outward look,
Catalogued its properties: sulphur, sagas, geysers
And sphagnum moss; rocks rising in snow-ribbed tiers
Over fiords. A slate sky. But now we have arrived
By night, lucky and thankful to have survived,
I was not ready for this blaze of light,
A shield over the harbour, nor the moon like a kite
Tying its lemon rays to the muzzled mountains,
Laying out for inspection what the bay contains;
Destroyers, sweepers, oilers and corvettes.
And there, coming to greet us, the silhouettes
Of launches, their wakes throwing up phosphorus
Like a northern champagne. They'll have sailing orders for us:
And before even checking what I imagine
Dawn here to look like, spilling over the snowline
And bald rock the crimson canister of the sun,
We shall be off, the convoy behind us in echelon.

Alan Ross

Destroyers in the Arctic

Camouflaged, they detach lengths of sea and sky
When they move; offset, speed and direction are a lie.

Everything is grey anyway; ships, water, snow, faces.
Flanking the convoy, we rarely go through our paces:

But sometimes on tightening waves at night they wheel
Drawing white moons on strings from dripping keel.

Cold cases them, like ships in glass; they are formal,
Not real, except in adversity. Then, too, have to seem normal.

At dusk they intensify dusk, strung out, non-committal:
Waves spill from our wake, crêpe paper magnetized by gun-metal.

They breathe silence, less solid than ghosts, ruminative
As the Arctic breaks up on their sides and they sieve

Moisture into mess-decks. Heat is cold-lined there,
Where we wait for a torpedo and lack air.

Repetitive of each other, imitating the sea's lift and fall,
On the wings of the convoy they indicate rehearsal.

Merchantmen move sideways, with the gait of crustaceans,
Round whom like eels escorts take up their stations.

Landfall, Murmansk; but starboard now a lead-coloured
Island, Jan Mayen. Days identical, hoisted like sails, blurred.

Counters moved on an Admiralty map, snow like confetti
Covers the real us. We dream we are counterfeits tied to our jetty.

But cannot dream long; the sea curdles and sprawls,
Liverishly real, and merciless all else away from us falls.

Kingsley Amis

Belgian Winter

The plains awkwardly revealed by history,
War in the wrong place, the usual day,
Stupid in the dignity of shot,
Blunt the ambitions, make all speak alone.
Martyrdom is a thing of cities, not
The country of the dull; the beautiful
And eloquent showily marked for death;
Unmoving faces are destined to live long.

From my window stretches the earth, containing wrecks:
The burrowing tank, the flat grave, the
Lorry with underside showing, like a dead rabbit.
The trees that smear all light into a mess;
World of one tone, stolid with fallen snow.
Here is the opaque ice, the humdrum winter,
The splintered houses suddenly come upon
Left over from wounds that pierced a different people.

But there are people here, unable to understand,
Randy for cigarettes, moving hands too
Jerky to move in love; their women matrons, their daughters
Frantically guarded or whores with lovely teeth;
The sons come from somewhere else, fair of skin;
The children have thick white socks and an English laugh,
Bearers of flowers, quiet and pointlessly clean,
Showing their parents up, not easily amused.

Behind is the city, a garnished London, a Paris
That has no idea how to live, of Chirico squares;
A feast of enemies, the stranger entertained
With opera and lesbian exhibitions,
Assurances of enjoyment and sameness; the pubs
Like railway buffets, bare and impersonal.
Smiles exclude the hypothesis of starving, but
The conqueror is advised to keep to the boulevards.

Then if history had a choice, he would point his cameras
Oh yes anywhere but here, any time but now;
But this is given us as the end of something
Important, something we must try to remember;
No music or kisses we want attend the fade-out,
Only a same sky or an embarrassing room,
Lust for something and a lust for no one,
Aloneness of crowds, infidelity, love's torture.

6—The Dead

Keith Douglas

Dead Men

Tonight the moon inveigles them
to love; they infer from her gaze
her tacit encouragement.
Tonight the white dresses and the jasmin scent
in the streets. I in another place
see the white dresses glimmer like moths. Come

to the west, out of that trance, my heart –
here the same hours have illumined
sleepers who are condemned or reprieved
and those whom their ambitions have deceived;
the dead men whom the wind
powders till they are like dolls; they tonight

rest in the sanitary earth perhaps
or where they died, no one has found them
or in their shallow graves the wild dog
discovered and exhumed a face or a leg
for food: the human virtue round them
is a vapour tasteless to a dog's chops.

All that is good of them, the dog consumes.
You would not know now the mind's flame is gone
more than the dog knows; you would forget
but that you see your own mind burning yet
and till you stifle in the ground will go on
burning the economical coal of your dreams.

Then leave the dead in the earth, an organism
not capable of resurrection, like mines,
less durable than the metal of a gun,
a casual meal for a dog, nothing but the bone
so soon. But tonight no lovers see the lines
of the moon's face as the lines of cynicism.

And the wise man is the lover
who is his planetary love resolves
without the traction of reason or time's control
and the wild dog finding meat in a hole
is a philosopher. The prudent mind resolves
on the lover's or the dog's attitude forever.

Hamish Henderson

Seven Good Germans

*The track running between Mekili and Tmimi was at one time a kind
of no-man's-land. British patrolling was energetic and there were
numerous brushes with German and Italian elements. El Eleba lies
about half-way along this track.*

Of the swaddies
who came to the desert with Rommel
There were few who had heard (or would hear) of El Eleba.
They recce'd,
or acted as medical orderlies
or patched up their tanks in the camouflaged workshops
and never gave a thought to a place like El Eleba.

To get there, you drive into the blue, take a bearing
and head for damn-all. Then you're there. And where are you?

– Still, of some few who did cross our path at El Eleba
there are seven who bide under their standing crosses.

The first a Lieutenant.
When the medicos passed him
for service overseas, he had jotted in a note-book

*to the day and the hour   keep me steadfast   there is only
the decision and the will
              the rest has no importance*

The second a Corporal.
He had been in the Legion
and had got one more chance to redeem his lost honour.
What he said was
          *Listen here, I'm fed up with your griping –
If you want extra rations, go get 'em from Tommy!
You're green, that's your trouble. Dodge the column, pass the buck
and scrounge all you can – that's our law in the Legion.
You know Tommy's got 'em ... He's got mineral waters,
and beer, and fresh fruit in that white crinkly paper*

and God knows what all! Well, what's holding you back?
Are you windy or what?
Christ, you 'old Afrikaners'!
If you're wanting the eats, go and get 'em from Tommy!

The third had been a farm-hand in the March of Silesia
and had come to the desert as fresh fodder for machine-guns.
His dates are inscribed on the files, and on the cross-piece.

The fourth was a lance-jack.
He had trusted in Adolf
while working as a chemist in the suburb of Spandau.
His loves were his 'cello, and the woman who had born him
two daughters and a son. He had faith in the Endsieg.
THAT THE NEW REICH MAY LIVE prayed the flyleaf of his
    Bible.

The fifth a mechanic.
All the honour and glory,
The siege of Tobruk and the conquest of Cairo
meant as much to that Boche as the Synod of Whitby.
Being wise to all this, he had one single headache,
which was, how to get back to his sweetheart (called Ilse).
– He had said
Can't the Tommy wake up and get weaving?
If he tried, he could put our whole Corps in the bag.
May God damn this Libya and both of its palm-trees!

The sixth was a Pole
– or to you, a Volksdeutscher –
who had put off his nation to serve in the Wehrmacht.
He siegheiled, and talked of 'the dirty Polacken',
and said what he'd do if let lose among Russkis,
His mates thought that, though 'just a polnischer Schweinhund'
he was not a bad bloke.
On the morning concerned
he was driving a truck with mail, petrol and rations.

The MP on duty shouted five words of warning.
He nodded
      laughed
            revved
                 and drove straight for Eleba
not having quite got the chap's Styrian lingo.

The seventh a young swaddy.
              Riding cramped in a lorry
to death along the road which winds eastwards to Halfaya
he had written three verses in appeal against his sentence
which soften for an hour the anger of Lenin.

    Seven poor bastards
    dead in African deadland
(tawny tousled hair under the issue blanket)
      wie einst Lili
    dead in African deadland
           einst Lili Marleen

Keith Douglas

Vergissmeinicht

Three weeks gone and the combatants gone,
returning over the nightmare ground
we found the place again, and found
the soldier sprawling in the sun.

The frowning barrel of his gun
overshadowing. As we came on
that day, he hit my tank with one
like the entry of a demon.

Look. Here in the gunpit spoil
the dishonoured picture of his girl
who has put: *Steffi. Vergissmeinicht*
in a copybook gothic script.

We see him almost with content
abased, and seeming to have paid
and mocked at by his own equipment
that's hard and good when he's decayed.

But she would weep to see today
how on his skin the swart flies move;
the dust upon the paper eye
and the burst stomach like a cave.

For here the lover and the killer are mingled
who had one body and one heart.
And death who had the soldier singled
has done the lover mortal hurt.

Alun Lewis

Song   (*On seeing dead bodies floating off the Cape*)

The first month of his absence
I was numb and sick
And where he'd left his promise
Life did not turn or kick.
The seed, the seed of love was sick.

The second month my eyes were sunk
In the darkness of despair,
And my bed was like a grave
And his ghost was lying there.
And my heart was sick with care.

The third month of his going
I thought I heard him say
'Our course, deflected slightly
On the thirty-second day –'
The tempest blew his words away.

And he was lost among the waves,
The ship rolled helpless in the sea,
The fourth month of his voyage
He shouted grievously
'Beloved, do not think of me.'

To flying fish like kingfishers
Skin the sea's bewildered crests,
The whales blow steaming fountains,
The sea-gulls have no nests
Where my lover sways and rests.

We never thought to buy or sell
The life that blooms or withers in the leaf,
And I'll not stir, so he sleeps well,
Though cell by cell the coral reef
Builds an eternity of grief.

But oh! the drag and dullness of my Self;
The turning seasons wither in my head;
All this slowness, all this hardness,
The nearness that is waiting in my bed,
The gradual self-effacement of the dead.

Bernard Gutteridge

Gold Mohar

A dark green lawn, a swathe
Of luteous bloom yet lingers.
And then this silver nicety
Of accurate trembling fingers.
The old tree with a lovely name
Graceful as its poised branches,
Old arms reaching to finicky twigs
The wind collects and launches,
A thin fern-like periphery.

You dead, my friends, still stay
Like this exquisite tree
My eyes must leave, heraldic
Flowering I will not see
Scald in April with crimson
Showers of petals. Then lie
There among its roots and blossom.
Your graces to the moonstone sky
It will yearly repay.

Bernard Gutteridge

The Enemy Dead

The dead are always searched.
It's not a man, the blood-soaked
Mess of rice and flesh and bones
Whose pockets you flip open;
And these belongings are only
The counterpart to scattered ball
Or the abandoned rifle.

Yet later the man lives.
His postcard of a light blue
Donkey and sandy minarets
Reveals a man at last.
'Object – the panther mountains!
Two – a tired soldier of Kiku!
Three – my sister the bamboo sigh!'

Then again the man dies.
And only what he has seen
And felt, loved and feared
Stays as a hill, a soldier, a girl:
Are printed in the skeleton
Whose white bones divide and float away
Like nervous birds in the sky.

R. N. Currey

Burial Flags

Here with the desert so austere that only
Flags live, plant out your flags upon the wind,
Red tattered bannerets that mark a lonely
    Grave in the sand;

A crude oblong of stone to hold some mortal
Remains against a jackal's rooting paws,
Painted with colour-wash to look like marble
    Through the heat-haze;

Roofed casually with corrugated iron
Held up by jutting and uneven poles;
The crooked flagpoles tied to a curved headstone
    Carved with symbols –

Stars and new moon that are the only flowers
To grow out of this naked earth and sky,
Except these flags that through the windy hours
    Bloom steadily,

Dull red, the faded red of women's garments
Carried on sudden camels past the sky –
Red strips of cloth that ride the dusty heavens
    Untiringly.

Drummond Allison

A Funeral Oration

For Douglas whom the cloud and eddy rejected,
though clad in dark Wellington he had deserved
Perpetual fellowship with those aerish beasts
Whom the eloquent eagle introduced to Chaucer;
But now the North Sea separates his bones
– Douglas who cocked an incessant snook at Death –
And crab and plaice make love wherever his soul
Shrived by a Messerschmidt cannon began to be sand,
They make light of his non-watertight prowess.

For Robert whom the wrath of the Atlantic
And untiring fire proved by the mouth of the River
Plate, but later the Mediterranean
Whose vaults he visited tricked and shut securely
in, and he penetrates forever the palaces of Atlantis.

For Colin last seen within sight of Greenland,
Who disagreed with all the gods and went down
The gradual stairs of the sea with the *Hood* until
He could have used vacated shells for tankards
A vigorous white worm for a cigarette
And girl friends having swords upon their snouts.

Herbert Corby

Two Sonnets

I

He was the mutual mother when we cursed
training in blizzards, facing the vicious snow;
Rex, who'd been a laughing fool at first,
tinkling with Chopin, hissing a line from Poe.
He was the careless one, who, at sloping arms
entices the sergeant to his loudest words,
yet the one who strolled across the forbidden farms,
populous with bulls, to listen to the birds.
The cocky one who wore his cap askew,
who, bayoneting the straw, would apologize,
his eyes aslant: the one who always knew
sly tricks for proving truth in all his lies.
He was our friend, loyal yet fancy-free.
He now lies dead and wrecked in Germany.

II

Jerome again was such another. Once
forming squad he marched on to the sand
returning with smiling eyes, gritty with puns,
saying he'd a sergeant jellyfish in his hand.
On guard he'd start, and make a bayonet poke
low down, and say he'd seen a mouse:
he'd halt the local mayor like a stroke,
present arms to the bland indifferent cows.
In Lancashire we left him. In the town
we'd drunk our healths for this life and the next
and Jerome stood away from us, his frown
judging our aled goodbyes, far-off, perplexed.
Set in his turret he'd seen the whole sky alter,
the Dornier swoop oddly to the sea, and falter.

Paul Dehn

Killed in Action

We seek the same prey, Scavenger,
With hooked and lonely hands.
To-night at your long table
Sit six of my friends.

Under the star-shells
Glisten and decay
The six grave faces
I loved as a boy.

Yours, now, that once were mine,
Rib, wrist and hair.
Is there at your long table,
Prince, an empty chair?

Gavin Ewart

When a Beau Goes In

When a Beau goes in,
Into the drink,
It makes you think,
Because, you see, they always sink
But nobody says 'Poor lad'
Or goes about looking sad
Because, you see, it's war,
It's the unalterable law.

Although it's perfectly certain
The pilot's gone for a Burton
And the observer too
It's nothing to do with you
And if they both should go
To a land where falls no rain nor hail nor driven snow –
Here, there or anywhere,
Do you suppose *they* care?

You shouldn't cry
Or say a prayer or sigh.
In the cold sea, in the dark,
It isn't a lark
But it isn't Original Sin –
It's just a Beau going in.

John Pudney

For Johnny

Do not despair
For Johnny-head-in-air;
He sleeps as sound
As Johnny underground.

Fetch out no shroud
For Johnny-in-the-cloud;
And keep your tears
For him in after years.

Better by far
For Johnny-the-bright-star,
To keep your head,
And see his children fed.

Paul Dehn

Lament for a Sailor

Here, where the night is clear as sea-water
And stones are white and the sticks are spars,
Swims on a windless, mackerel tide
The dolphin moon in a shoal of stars.

Here, in the limbo, where moths are spinners
And clouds like hulls drift overhead,
Move we must for our colder comfort,
I the living and you the dead.

Each on our way, my ghost, my grayling,
You to the water, the land for me;
I am the fat-knuckled, noisy diver
But you are the quietest fish in the sea.

7—History's Thread

Drummond Allison

We Shall Have Company

If soon by violence and political police, if soon our class
Is to be flung through doors it opened with such care,
If the cream telephones are to be answered
By black slouchcaps and oilstained dungarees
While from directors' chairs the shop-steward runs
Europe and love and every watchful author;
Till State itself can wither, first unclench,
Till Nature's cheques
Bear signatures appended by another;

Or if our nation is erased without a smudge,
Seamen and colonists and sad
Clerks in the suburbs who denied their sorrow,
Playwrights and princes and gladly unemployed,
Miners and centre-forwards, clergy proud
Of God and their son; if under similar standards
I too go down with some self-conscious laugh
Like one too late
Discovering the examiners were serious;

We shall have company who haunt the highway's ghost
Which now the painstaking Atlantic gloatingly grinds.
We shall ride out on quaggers, on mastodon and mammoth,
Pat old triceratops in passing, stroke the dinosaur.
Sung to by pterodactyls we shall strew
Food for the roc, the great auk and the moa.
Giant sloth and sabretooth shall grow tame for us,
Neanderthal and Piltdown will be willing guides to us
And ichthyosaurus wallow no longer malevolent.

Julian Symons

Gladstone

'It is so easy to write, but to write honestly nearly impossible'—

Gladstone: Diary 1896

The images break upon a sad day.
I think of a friend recently killed
Whose death leaves me without understanding,
Bitterness or anger. The delicate hours
Wash over my head like waves of bells
Clanging. I look up to see
The great stone presence of the orator.

He wavers like a dream in front of the window
And through him I see trees in bud.
His raised hand asks for silence, he fills
The room with an odour of purity.
The spotlight is focused, music plays,
I sit forward expectant, his voice begins.

I forget what he means but remember the words,
Or lose the words but remember the meaning.
I forget. I forget. The voice goes on,
Brilliant, tireless, unendurable,
The phrases cohere and separate
And become indistinct, they form a web
Of words that envelope me, the dropped
Phrases are appropriate as a song:

Though everything I did was always wrong
My aims were virtuous, my will was strong

I had no vanity but simply knew
Those who opposed me were not good or true

When I got up to speak all the ideal
And abstract thoughts took flesh and were made real

Only sometimes at night I heard a voice
That said man's fate does not result from choice,
And economy of force is what destroys.

In the cold watch of early spring
His words and image hang in the room,
That ghastly white-haired phantom of
Another time, outside the trees
Waving slowly in the breeze
And thoughts of my friend who died
For a cause in which he did not believe,

All these make up a pattern against which
I oppose in my own life gestures
And thought's free movement merely. For my friend,
Killed in the third year of the second capitalist war
There are now no Liberal ghosts and no reproaches,
But for me the spring advances and the unlimited
Areas of conflict remain outside, the problems of action
And honesty are still unreconciled.

F. T. Prince

Soldiers Bathing

The sea at evening moves across the sand.
Under a reddening sky I watch the freedom of a band
Of soldiers who belong to me. Stripped bare
For bathing in the sea, they shout and run in the warm air;
Their flesh, worn by the trade of war, revives
And my mind towards the meaning of it strives.

All's pathos now. The body that was gross,
Rank, ravenous, disgusting in the act or in repose,
All fever, filth and sweat, its bestial strength
And bestial decay, by pain and labour grows at length
Fragile and luminous. 'Poor bare forked animal,'
Conscious of his desires and needs and flesh that rise and fall,
Stands in the soft air, tasting after toil
The sweetness of his nakedness: letting the sea-waves coil
Their frothy tongues about his feet, forgets
His hatred of the war, its terrible pressure that begets
A machinery of death and slavery,
Each being a slave and making slaves of others; finds that he
Remembers his old freedom in a game
Mocking himself, and comically mimics fear and shame.

He plays with death and animality;
And reading in the shadows of his pallid flesh, I see
The idea of Michelangelo's cartoon
Of soldiers bathing, breaking off before they were half done
At some sortie of the enemy, and episode
Of the Pisan wars with Florence. I remember how he showed
Their muscular limbs that clamber from the water,
And heads that turn across the shoulder, eager for the slaughter,
Forgetful of their bodies that are bare,
And hot to buckle on and use the weapons lying there.
– And I think too of the theme another found
When, shadowing men's bodies on a sinister red ground,
Another Florentine, Pollaiuolo,
Painted a naked battle: warriors, straddle, hacked the foe,
Dug their bare toes into the ground and slew

The brother-naked man who lay between their feet and drew
His lips back from his teeth in a grimace.

They were Italians who knew war's sorrow and disgrace
And showed the thing suspended, stripped: a theme
Born out of the experience of war's horrible extreme
Beneath a sky where even the air flows
With lacrimae Christi. For that rage, that bitterness, those blows,
That hatred of the slain, what could they be
But indirectly or directly a commentary
On the Crucifixion? And the picture burns
With indignation and pity and despair by turns,
Because it is the obverse of the scene
Where Christ hangs murdered, stripped, upon the Cross. I mean,
That is the explanation of its rage.

And we too have our bitterness and pity that engage
Blood, spirit, in this war. But night begins,
Night of the mind: who nowadays is conscious of our sins?
Though every human deed concerns our blood,
And even we must know, what nobody had understood,
That some great love is over all we do,
And that is what has driven us to this fury, for so few
Can suffer all the terror of that love:
The terror of that love has set us spinning in this groove
Greased with our blood.

           These dry themselves and dress,
Combing their hair, forget the fear and shame of nakedness.
Because to love is frightening we prefer
The freedom of our crimes. Yet, as I drink the dusky air,
I feel a strange delight that fills me full,
Strange gratitude, as if evil itself were beautiful,
And kiss the wound in thought, while in the west
I watch a streak of red that might have issued from Christ's breast.

Alun Lewis

Westminster Abbey

Discoloured lights slant from the high rose window
Upon the sightseers and the faithful
And those who shelter from the rain this Sunday.
The clergy in their starched white surplices
Send prayers like pigeons circling overhead
Seeking the ghostly hands that give them bread.

The togaed statesmen on their scribbled plinths
Stand in dull poses, dusty as their fame
Crammed in the chapter of a schoolboy's book;
Their eyes have lost their shrewd and fallible look.

Kneeling by Gladstone is a girl who sobs.
Something profounder than the litany
Moves in the dark beneath the restless steps
Of this pale swirl of human flux.
Soft fingers touch the worn marmoreal stone.
The pale girl reaches out for what has gone.

The thin responsions falter in the air.
Only the restless footsteps hurry on,
Escaping that which was in the beginning,
is now, and ever shall be.
                          – See, the girl
Adjusts her fashionable veil.
The vergers clack their keys, the soldiers go,
The white procession shuffles out of sight.

The incubus is shifted to the stars,
The flux is spun and drifted through the night,
And no one stays within that holy shell
To know if that which IS be good or ill.

Alun Lewis

Corfe Castle

Framed in a jagged window of grey stones
These wooded pastures have a dream-like air.
You thrill with disbelief
To see the cattle move in a green field.

Grey Purbeck houses by the sun deceived
Sleep with the easy consciences of the old;
The swathes are sweet on slopes new harvested;
Householders prune their gardens, count the slugs;
The beanrows flicker flowers red as flames.

Those to whom life is a picture card
Get their cheap thrill here where the centuries stand
A thrusting mass transfigured by the sun
Reeling above the streets and crowing farms.
The rooks and skylarks are okay for sound,
The toppling bastions innocent with stock.

Love grows impulsive here: the best forget;
The failures of the earth will try again.
She would go back to him if he but asked.
The tawny thrush is silent; when he sings
His silence is fulfilled. Who wants to talk
As trippers do? Yet, love,
Before we go be simple as this grass,
Lie rustling for this last time in my arms.
Quicken the dying island with your breath.

Keith Douglas

Aristocrats
'I think I am becoming a God'

The noble horse with courage in his eye
clean in the bone, looks up at a shellburst:
away fly the images of the shires
but he puts the pipe back in his mouth.

Peter was unfortunately killed by an 88:
it took his leg away, he died in the ambulance.
I saw him crawling on the sand; he said
It's most unfair, they've shot my foot off.

How can I live among this gentle
obsolescent breed of heroes, and not weep?
Unicorns, almost,
for they are falling into two legends
in which their stupidity and chivalry
are celebrated. Each, fool and hero, will be an immortal.

The plains were their cricket pitch
and in the mountains the tremendous drop fences
brought down some of the runners. Here then
under the stones and earth they dispose themselves,
I think with their famous unconcern.
It is not gunfire I hear but a hunting horn.

Roy Fuller

Autumn 1942

Season of rains: the horizon like an illness
Daily retreating and advancing: men
Swarming on aircraft: things that leave their den
And prowl the suburbs: cries in the starlit stillness –

Into the times' confusion such sharp captions
Are swiftly cut, as symbols give themselves
To poets, though the convenient nymphs and elves
They know fall sadly short of their conceptions.

I see giraffes that lope, half snake, half steed,
A slowed-up film; the soft bright zebra race,
Unreal as rocking horses; and the face –
A solemn mandarin's – of the wildebeest.

And sometimes in the mess the men and their
Pathetic personal trash become detached
From what they move on; and my days are patched
With newspapers about the siege-like war.

Should I be asked to speak the truth, these are
What I should try to explain, and leave unsaid
Our legacy of failure from the dead.
The silent fate of our provincial star.

But what can be explained? The animals
Are what you make of them, are words, are visions,
And they for us are moving in dimensions
Impertinent to use or watch at all.

And of the men there's nothing to be said:
Only events, with which they wrestle, can
Transfigure them or make them other than
Things to be loved or hated and soon dead.

It is the news at which I hesitate,
That glares authentically between the bars
Of style and lies, and holds enough of fears
And history, and is not too remote.

And tells me that the age is thus: chokes back
My private suffering, the ghosts of nature
And of the mind: it says the human features
Are mutilated, have a dreadful lack.

It half convinces me that some great faculty,
Like hands, has been eternally lost and all
Our virtues now are the high and horrible
Ones of a streaming wound which heals in evil.

Roy Fuller

Harbour Ferry

The oldest and simplest thoughts
Rise with the antique moon:
How she enamels men
And artillery under her sphere,
Eyelids and hair and throats
Rigid in love and war;
How this has happened before.

And how the lonely man
Raises his head and shudders
With a brilliant sense of the madness,
The age and shape of his planet,
Wherever his human hand,
Whatever his set of tenets,
The long and crucial minute.

Tonight the moon has risen
Over a quiet harbour,
Through twisted iron and labour,
Lighting the half-drowned ships.
Oh surely the fatal chasm
is closer, the furious steps
Swifter? The silver drips

From the angle of the wake;
The moon is flooding the faces.
The moment is over; the forces
Controlling lion nature
Look out of the eyes and speak:
Can you believe in a future
Left only to rock and creature?

Roy Fuller

The Middle of a War

My photograph already looks historic.
The promising youthful face, the matelot's collar,
Say 'This one is remembered for a lyric.
His place and period – nothing could be duller.'

Its position is already indicated –
The son or brother in the album; pained
The expression and the garments dated,
His fate so obviously pre-ordained.

The original turns away; as horrible thoughts,
Loud fluttering aircraft slope above his head
At dusk. The ridiculous empires break like biscuits.

Ah, life has been abandoned by the boats –
Only the trodden island and the dead
Remain, and the once inestimable caskets.

Charles Causley

Conversation in Gibraltar 1943

We sit here, talking of Barea and Lorca
Meeting the iron eye of the Spanish clock.
We have cut, with steel bows, the jungle of salt-water,
Sustaining the variable sea-fevers of home and women,
To walk the blazing ravine
Of the profitable Rock.

We hold, in our pockets, no comfortable return tickets:
Only the future, gaping like some hideous fable.
The antique Mediterranean of history and Alexander,
The rattling galley and the young Greek captains
Are swept up and piled
Under the table.

We have walked to Europa and looked east to the invisible island,
The bitter rock biting the heel through the shoe-leather.
Rain's vague infantry, the Levant, parachutes on the stone lion
And soon, soon, under our feet and the thin steel deck
We shall be conscious of miles of perpendicular sea,
And the Admiralty weather.

R. N. Currey

Dam

I feel uneasy living beneath this dam.
The walls reach up to hold the infinite sky,
The hidden weight of waters, the poised hills –
And all the unguessed future, fragile walls
Buttressed by relics of a feudal past
And some two centuries' power, a world propped up
By boards that curve and strain; through sizable cracks
The waters splash and spray along the rim.

O lovely world of morning-plumaged skies
And wide gun-metal waters; teal and snipe –
The whirring fighters and formation flights
Of poised out-reaching bombers; as I lie here,
Under the atlas-shoulders of this dam,
I hear the waters walk above my head!

Keith Douglas

Time eating

Ravenous Time has flowers for his food
in Autumn, yet can cleverly make good
each petal; devours animals and men,
but for ten dead he can create ten.

If you enquire how secretly you've come
to mansize from the smallness of a stone
it will appear his efforts made you rise
so gradually to your proper size.

But as he makes he eats; the very part
where he began, even the elusive heart,
Time's ruminative tongue will wash
and slow juice masticate all flesh.

That volatile huge intestine holds
material and abstract in its folds:
thought and ambition melt and even the world
will alter, in that catholic belly curled.

But Time, who ate my love, you cannot make
such another; you who can remake
the lizard's tail and the bright snakeskin
cannot, cannot. That you gobbled in
too quick, and though you brought me from a boy
you can make no more of me only destroy.

8—The Americans

Richard Eberhart

A Ceremony by the Sea

Unbelievable as an antique ritual,
With touch of Salamis and Marathon,
Through what visions of rebirth and death
At Atlantic's blue, hot, and sparkling edge –

War's head is up, war's bloody head, –
The thirtieth of May beats through America
With here the band, the boardwalk, and the speeches
Masking with blaze the parted beach crowds.

The traffic still restless, the loudspeaker proud,
Young couples in swimsuits strolling hand in hand
Beyond the crowd, self-interested, not attending.
But comes a hush like shimmer of summer over all,

With solemn tones the names are called, John Pettingill,
Roger Ashcroft, Timothy O'Shaughnessy, Patrick
O'Shaughnessy, Olaf Erikson, Alan Hieronymus,
William Henry Cabe, Neil Campbell, Victor Giampetruzzi . . .

Long pauses after each name, as mother or father,
Grandfather or grandmother, uncle or brother
Awkwardly walks through the entangling sand
With sheaf or wreath of flowers to the flower-waggon,

Burgeoning with brightness beneath the bandstand.
The newly dead! The young, the dead far away,
In the strange young reality of their war deaths
Too young for this austere memorial.

The last name is called, the last flower is funded,
As people stand in the daze of the actual,
Then eight young men of the Army and Navy,
Almost naked, strong swimmers of the tides of life,

Their muscles blending in among the flowers,
Take up, four each, the flower-twined ropes.

Like a mad disturbance, hafts to the hilt of earth air,
Eighty Corsairs plummet out of the sky

From high inland down over the bandstand,
Four abreast, flash out over the sand
Over the ocean, and up easily and turn.
The deafening noise and closeness is a spell.

Then the flower waggon by the stalwart ones slowly
Through the crowd begins to go to the sea,
And as it draws, the ocean opens up its heart
To the heavy hearts of mourners by the sea's edge.

These, all kinds and conditions of men,
Thereafter follow across that bright, that transient course
As they would pay their tribute to the waves,
To the justice unaccountable of final things,

Followers of flowers; the gorgeous waggon-coffin
Drawing the blood out of the crowd, slow-passing it.
And lastly I saw an aged Italian couple
Too old to stumble through that catching sand,

The backs of their bodies bent like man himself,
Ancient as Marathon or as Salamis,
New and ancient as is America,
Diminish with laborious march toward the water.

From the platform funeral music played
In dirge that broke upon purged air
While now in mid distance, far by the shore, the new fated
Stood; then the powerful, the graceful youths

Like gods who would waft to far horizons
Drew the waggon in, which then a boat of flowers
They swam with, dim swan on the searoad.
A waiting gunboat fired the last salute.

Richard Eberhart

The Fury of Aerial Bombardment

You would think the fury of aerial bombardment
Would rouse God to relent; the infinite spaces
Are still silent. He looks on shock-pried faces.
History, even, does not know what is meant.

You would feel that after so many centuries
God would give man to repent; yet he can kill
As Cain could, but with multitudinous will,
No farther advanced than in his ancient furies.

Was man made stupid to see his own stupidity?
Is God by definition indifference, beyond us all?
Is the eternal truth man's fighting soul
Wherein the Beast ravens in its own avidity?

Of Van Wettering I speak, and Averill,
Names on a list, whose faces I do not recall
But they are gone to early death, who late in school
Distinguished the belt feed lever from the belt holding pawl.

Randall Jarrell

The Death of the Ball Turret Gunner

From my mother's sleep I fell into the State,
And I hunched in its belly till my wet fur froze.
Six miles from earth, loosed from its dream of life,
I woke to black flak and the nightmare fighters.
When I died they washed me out of the turret with a hose.

Randall Jarrell

A Camp in the Prussian Forest

I walk beside the prisoners to the road.
Load on puffed load,
Their corpses, stacked like sodden wood,
Lie barred or galled with blood

By the charred warehouse. No one comes to-day
In the old way
To knock the fillings from their teeth;
The dark, coned, common wreath

Is plaited for their grave – a kind of grief.
The living leaf
Clings to the planted profitable
Pine if it is able;

The boughs sigh, mile on green, calm, breathing mile,
From this dead file
The planners ruled for them . . . One year
They sent a million here:

Here men were drunk like water, burnt like wood.
The fat of good
and evil, the breast's star of hope
were rendered into soap.

I paint the star I sawed from yellow pine –
And plant the sign
In soil that does not yet refuse
Its usual Jews

Their first asylum. But the white, dwarfed star –
This dead white star –
Hides nothing, pays for nothing; smoke
Fouls it, a yellow joke,

The needles of the wreath are chalked with ash,
A filmy trash
Litters the black woods with the death
Of men; and one last breath

Curls from the monstrous chimney ... I laugh aloud
Again and again;
The star laughs from its rotting shroud
Of flesh. O star of men!

Randall Jarrell

The Dead Wingman

Seen on the sea; no sign; no sign; no sign
In the black firs and terraces of hills
Ragged in mist. The cone narrows; snow
Glares from the bleak walls of a crater. No.
Again the houses jerk like paper, turn,
And the surf streams by; a port of toys
is starred with its fires and faces; but no sign.

In the level light, over the fiery shores,
The plane circles stubbornly: the eyes distending
With hatred and misery and longing, stare
Over the blackening ocean for a corpse.
The fires are guttering; the dials fall,
A long dry shudder climbs along his spine,
His fingers tremble; but his hand unchanging stare
Moves unacceptingly: *I have a friend.*

The fires are grey; no star, no sign
Winks from the breathing darkness of the carrier
Where the pilot circles for his wingman; where,
Gliding above the cities' shells, a stubborn eye
Among the embers of the nations, achingly
Tracing the circles of that worn, unchanging *No* –
The lives' long war, lost war – the pilot sleeps.

Howard Nemerov

Redeployment

They say the war is over. But water still
Comes bloody from the taps, and my pet cat
In his disorder vomits worms which crawl
Swiftly away. Maybe they leave the house.
These worms are white, and flecked with the cat's blood.

The war may be over. I know a man
Who keeps a pleasant souvenir, he keeps
A soldier's dead blue eyeballs that he found
Somewhere – hard as chalk, and blue as slate.
He clicks them in his pocket while he talks.

And now there are cockroaches in the house,
They get slightly drunk on DDT,
Are fast, hard, shifty – can be drowned but not
Without you hold them under quite some time.
People say the Mexican kind can fly.

The end of the war. I took it quietly
Enough. I tried to wash the dirt out of
My hair and from under my fingernails,
I dressed in clean white clothes and went to bed.
I heard the dust falling between the walls.

Howard Nemerov

A Fable of the War

The full moon is partly hidden by cloud,
The snow that fell when we came off the boat
Has stopped by now, and it is turning colder.
I pace the platform under the blue lights,
Under a frame of glass and emptiness
In a station whose name I do not know.

Suddenly, passing the known and unknown
Bowed faces of my company, the sad
And potent outfit of the armed, I see
That we are dead. By stormless Acheron
We stand easy, and the occasional moon
Strikes terribly from steel and bone alike.

Our flesh, I see, was too corruptible
For the huge work of death. Only the blind
Crater of the eye can suffer well
The midnight cold of stations in no place,
And hold the tears of pity frozen that
They will implacably reflect on war.

But I have read that God let Solomon
Stand upright, although dead, until the temple
Should be raised up, that demons forced to the work
Might not revolt before the thing was done.
And the king stood, until a little worm
Had eaten through the stick he leaned upon.

So gentlemen – by greatcoat, cartridge belt
And helmet held together for the time –
In honourably enduring her we seek
The second death. Until the worm shall bite
To betray us, lean each man upon his gun
That the great work not falter but go on.

Louis Simpson

I Dreamed that in a City Dark as Paris

I dreamed that in a city dark as Paris
I stood alone in a deserted square.
The night was trembling with a violet
Expectancy. At the far edge it moved
And rumbled; on that flickering horizon
The guns were pumping colour in the sky.

There was the Front. But I was lonely here,
Left behind, abandoned by the army.
The empty city and the empty square
Was my inhabitation, my unrest.
The helmet with its vestige of a crest,
The rifle in my hands, long out of date,
The belt I wore, the trailing overcoat
and hobnail boots, were those of a *poilu.*
I was the man, as awkward as a bear.

Over the rooftops where cathedrals loomed
In speaking majesty, two aeroplanes
Forlorn as birds, appeared. Then growing large,
The German *Taube* and the *Nieuport Scout*,
They chased each other tumbling through the sky,
Till one streamed down on fire to the earth.

These wars have been so great, they are forgotten
Like the Egyptian dynasts. My confrere
In whose thick boots I stood, were you amazed
To wander through my brain four decades later
As I have wandered in a dream through yours?

The violence of waking life disrupts
The order of our death. Strange dreams occur,
For dreams are licensed as they never were.

Louis Simpson

The Battle

Helmet and rifle, pack and overcoat
Marched through a forest. Somewhere up ahead
Guns thudded. Like the circle of a throat
The night on every side was turning red.

They halted and they dug. They sank like moles
Into the clammy earth between the trees.
And soon the sentries, standing in their holes,
Felt the first snow. Their feet began to freeze.

At dawn the first shell landed with a crack.
Then shells and bullets swept the icy woods.
This lasted many days. The snow was black.
The corpses stiffened in their scarlet hoods.

Most clearly of that battle I remember
The tiredness in eyes, how hands looked thin
Around a cigarette, and the bright ember
Would pulse with all the life there was within.

Louis Simpson

Memories of a Lost War

The guns know what is what, but underneath
In fearful file
We go around burst boots and packs and teeth
That seem to smile.

The scene jags like a strip of celluloid,
A mortar fires,
Cinzano falls, Michelin is destroyed,
The man of tyres.

As darkness drifts like fog in from the sea
Somebody says
'We're digging in'. Look well, for this may be
The last of days.

Hot lightnings stitch the blind eye of the moon,
The thunder's blunt.
We sleep. Our dreams pass in a faint platoon
Toward the front.

Sleep well, for you are young. Each tree and bush
Drips with sweet dew,
And earlier than morning June's cool hush
Will waken you.

The riflemen will wake and hold their breath.
Though they may bleed
They will be proud awhile of something death
Still seems to need.

William Jay Smith

Morning at Arnhem

I

From the cassowary's beak come streaks of light,
Morning, and possibility.
In the countries of the north
Ice breaks, and breaking, blossoms forth
With possibility; and day abounds
In light and colour, colour, sounds.

II

In Holland there are tulips on the table,
A wind from the north on the grey stones
That breaks the heart, and sits upon the shoulder,
And turns the mill, the pine cones.

Waking below the level of the sea,
You wake in peace; the gardens look
Like roofs of palaces beneath the water,
And into the sea the land hooks.

In Holland there are tulips on the table,
A wind from the north on the grey stones
That breaks the heart, and turns, with the mill at cockcrow,
Over the quiet dead, the pine cones.

III

From the cassowary's beak come streaks of light;
A wrought iron angel mounts a weathervane; you might
Be anywhere in Europe now that night
Is over, and you see that life begins like this
In tragedy: in light that is entangled in the leaves,
And morning shaken from an angel's sleeves;

And you can turn to face the mouth
Of the great black lion of heaven,
The terrible, beautiful south.

Richard Wilbur

First Snow in Alsace

The snow came down last night like moths
Burned on the moon; it fell till dawn,
Covered the town with simple cloths.

Absolute snow lies rumpled on
What shellbursts scattered and deranged,
Entangled railings, crevassed lawn.

As if it did not know they'd changed,
Snow smoothly clasps the roofs of homes
Fear-gutted, trustless and estranged.

The ration stacks are milky domes;
Across the ammunition pile
The snow has climbed in sparkling combs.

You think: beyond the town a mile
Or two, this snowfall fills the eyes
Of soldiers dead a little while.

Persons and persons in disguise,
Walking the new air white and fine,
Trade glances quick with shared surprise.

At children's windows, heaped benign,
As always, winter shines the most,
And frost makes marvellous designs.

The night-guard coming from his post,
Ten first-snows back in thought, walks slow
And warms with him with a boyish boast:

He was the first to see the snow.

Richard Wilbur

Mined Country

They have gone into the grey hills quilled with birches,
Drag now their cannon up the chill mountains;
But it's going to be long before
Their war's gone for good.

I tell you it hits at childhood more than churches
Full up with sky or buried town fountains,
Rooms laid open or anything
Cut stone or cut wood,

Seeing the boys come swinging slow over the grass
(Like playing pendulum) their silver plates,
Stepping with care and listening
Hard for hid metal's cry.

It's rightly-called-chaste Belphoebe some would miss,
Some, calendar colts at Kentucky gates;
But the remotest would guess that
Some scheme's gone awry.

Danger is sunk in pastures, the woods are sly,
Ingenuity's covered with flowers!
We thought woods were wise but never
Implicated, never involved.

Cows in mid-munch go splattered over the sky;
Roses like brush-whores smile from bowers;
Shepherds must learn a new language; this
Isn't going to be quickly solved.

Sunshiny field grass, the woods floor, are so mixed up
With earlier trusts, you have to pick back
Far past all you have learned, to go
Disinherit the dumb child,

Tell him to trust things alike and never to stop
Emptying things, but not let them lack
Love in some manner restored; to be
Sure the whole world's wild.

Some autobiographical statements

Kingsley Amis

The war doesn't interest me much now, though it very much did at the time. I spent less than three and a half years of it in uniform, most of it as a lieutenant in the Royal Corps of Signals, fifteen months of it in the north-west Europe theatre, none of it under fire. The worst I had to put up with was an ordinary amount of malice from my superiors, a lot of physical exertion in the first months, and long bouts of hard work interrupted, and often accompanied, by boredom. I benefited in many more ways. The army got me away from home, sent me abroad for the first time, cured me of some of my sillier illusions, lessened my fear of strangers, helped on my sexual development, taught me how horrible people were when they had authority, and gave me material for a few poems (none of them any good), two stories and a novella. But I didn't enjoy it much at the time.

My feelings about the war as such were and are highly conventional, that it was very unpleasant, but altogether necessary; because the Germans had to be put down.

I think the whole experience changed me as much and as little as it changed most people. I don't think it changed my writing any more or any less than anything else has. If I'd seen action the story might possibly have been different. But, thank God, I didn't.

Jocelyn Brooke

As a writer I was deeply influenced by the war; not so much because the issues at stake made any great appeal to my imagination, but because the war succeeded in bouncing me out of a neurotic condition which had afflicted me through most of the 1930s. It is fashionable nowadays (and was in 1939) to mock at my namesake, Rupert Brooke's (no relation, by the way) 'Swimmers into cleanness leaping' and so forth; but the fact is that, for people like myself, this reaction could be as valid in 1939 (even if one was inclined to laugh at it) as it was in 1914. 'Cleanness', in 1939, was perhaps not quite the right word; but one was at least leaping into something different and difficult – like a winter bathe in the Serpentine.

During the 1930s I had been, in the literary sense, chronically constipated; trying to write, but fatally inhibited by my neuroses. After the war I sat down and wrote about fifteen books in the subsequent ten years; far too many. A lot were never published, and some of the ones that did get into print were doubtless very bad. But the war, distasteful and inconvenient though it was in many other respects, was in one sense 'good for me', bringing a sense of release and a renewed capacity to write the sort of stuff one had always wanted to write. This, of course, is no argument in favour of war, but I do rather doubt if I should ever have become a published author, either in prose or verse, if it hadn't been for the late Adolf Hitler.

Charles Causley

The war had a catalytic effect on me as a writer. Up till then, I'd lived the whole of my life in the small Cornish town where I was born. It was Hitler who pushed a subject under my nose; and the fact that poetry could be put together in one's head – when working at other jobs, lying half-asleep in a hammock, sitting in a bar – and written down, complete, on a bit of paper the way a play or novel or short-story couldn't, gave me a form.

To a young man of my age, health and lack of initiative, the only alternative to being called-up in 1939 was jail. I decided, out of a mixture of ignorance and fright, to opt for the Navy. I wanted to avoid the Army. I thought of my father, who had served as a private soldier in France during the 1914–18 war, and of the implications of some of the songs I'd heard from the returned soldiers. I had read Sassoon, Blunden, Graves, Owen. I also thought, with the Naval Barracks at Devonport only twenty-five miles away across the Tamar, that I should be able to get home for weekends. (I never did.)

I took a medical at the Plymouth City Museum and Art Gallery and put my name down for the navy as a writer – a sort of sea-going clerk. When I got my calling up papers in 1940 I went for training to an ex-Butlin's Holiday Camp, and became not a clerk but a coder. At first, nobody knew what this was. It turned out that we were in the communications branch and had to change coded messages into plain English, and vice versa; not a bad training for a poet, perhaps. For years after the war, if I came upon a jumble of letters and figures anywhere, I found myself absent-mindedly trying to make sense out of it.

At Butlin's we dressed up in seamen's rig and 'went ashore' in Skegness, under the impression that we were 'in' the navy. A couple of months later, in the roaring, granite, hell's-kitchen of the Royal Naval Barracks at Devonport, we realized that up to that moment we hadn't been. Here, at twenty-two, my education slowly began. I was drafted successively to a destroyer (Orkneys, South Atlantic), to a signal station in Gibraltar, to a training establishment near Liverpool (as an instructor), and to an aircraft-carrier which I joined in Belfast and finally left in Sydney, Australia. I became a civilian again in 1946.

I think the event that affected me more than anything else in those years was the fact that the companion who had left my home-town with me for the navy in 1940 was later lost in a convoy to Russia. From the moment I heard this news, I found myself haunted by the words in the twenty-fourth chapter of St Matthew: 'Then shall two be in the field; the one shall be taken, and the other left.' If my poetry is 'about' anything, it is this.

Robert Conquest

I enlisted in 1939, was commissioned in the Oxfordshire and Buckinghamshire Light Infantry in 1940 and was demobilized from it, as a captain, in 1946. I served for three years in its 4th Battalion, and was later detached to 125 Force. In 1944 I was flown in from Italy to Bulgaria. Afterwards, till the end of the war, I was attached to the Third Ukrainian Front.

Our generation had been brought up on the horrors of the First World War in a deeply war-hating mood. Nor was it only an influence of literature and ideas. The first war was deep in the family consciousness of many. At the same time, Nazism appeared a monstrous evil, and we had in principle no anti-war views as regards our own war. Thus, our opinions and our feelings were not well adjusted to each other.

In any case we had, from our reading and from our training, a perfectly clear and detailed idea of the personal possibilities. Thus, much of the effect of the war, as a trap for killing, was in anticipation. The most unpleasant prospect was the long set-piece infantry battle – Monte Cassino or the Reichwald; not so much death and danger, as death and danger when worn down by cold, fatigue and accumulated tension. And in particular the extreme limitations on freedom of action, the clockwork movement to timed barrages and so on. Long range patrols, well out of superior control, were exhilarating rather than not. I saw little action, and that not of a particularly dangerous or frightening sort. But there was always this expectation of finding oneself in a deadly situation at very short notice. The lottery which took one's friends and colleagues was always operating.

In addition, six years in the army, straight from university, is in itself a big slice of a young man's life. In most ways it was naturally detestable, and I am sure it strengthened and clarified an inborn dislike of authority and organisations in general, and an attachment to the principles of personal and civil liberty. Yet one was thrown into close contact with a wide range of people one would otherwise not have met, and from this one learnt charity and anger; patience and nostalgia.

Herbert Corby

My poetry has never attracted much attention anywhere, and it is probably true to say that my only worthwhile poems are those I wrote during my stint with the RAF. My style was developed in the thirties and has not changed. I have always written basically traditional verse which is easy to understand, and after I joined the RAF I just cobbled on, with a new range of personal experience to write about.

In the mid-thirties I was one of the Neuburg Group which included Dylan Thomas and Pamela Hansford Johnson. (The activities of this group are described by Jean Overton Fuller in *The Magical Dilemma of Victor Neuburg*.) Victor Neuburg was an unfailing source of encouragement to new poets and he published several of my poems in the Poets' Corner of *The Sunday Referee*, and later, in his own magazine *Comment*. When *Comment* ceased publication, there were very few editors who cared for my work, though I remember that Tambimuttu took a few poems of *Poetry London*, and Julian Symons printed one or two in his *Twentieth Century Verse*. But I was already carving out a future for myself as an unknown poet.

The war years, when I had a ready-made subject for my kind of verse, and the years immediately following demobilization, when the impetus gained from the war poems kept me writing, were the most productive. Since then, travel abroad (with the Foreign Service) has turned up new themes and ideas, but has not rekindled the urge to write which resulted in the RAF poems.

The war's effect on my writing (in intention at least) was to make me seek clarity and honesty: I had previously produced symbolism and pretentiousness. It also – in the Mediterranean Theatre, though this would probably not be so true of the Western Front – made one more sensitive and responsive to the qualities of sky and landscape, of the phenomenal world, in contrast both to the ruined cities and desolated farmlands and to one's own possible impending extinction. (On the other hand, it was a number of years before I was able to look at a country scene without seeing it in terms of fields of fire and dead ground.)

R. N. Currey

I approached the war from a different standpoint from many of my contemporaries. Having spent the first thirteen years of my life in the Transvaal and Natal, where nothing was a hundred years old and every road and building was an achievement, I could not take the cultural achievements of Europe for granted – could not see them as part of a corrupt society ripe for revolution. I stood outside the main literary stream, unmoved by the pylons and power-stations that were the symbols of the political propagandist poetry of the time: my own painful involvement with the machine came later.

I hated the idea of war as I hated the idea of revolution – as negative and destructive. I was old enough to remember something of the first war and I tended to think of the present war in terms of it. My mind ran on trenches. But though I wanted many kinds of reform, I did not have any strong political alignment to complicate my attitudes. Though I had, in fact, two chances of evading national service, I did not seriously consider them; the war, bad as it was, seemed the lesser evil, and perhaps at the back of my mind there was some remnant of the binding powers of a frontier tradition. I expected, as a reasonably fit academic person with no technical skills whatever, to be put in something non-technical like infantry. Instead, I found myself in Signals, struggling to learn the elements of electricity; at this time radar was being developed and I was soon passed on from there to Anti-Aircraft Artillery. I expected boredom, danger, regimentation, separation – and got them – but did not expect to be moved into the world of machines so many of my contemporaries had written about – usually from *outside*.

In *This Other Planet* I tried to express my sense of exile in this world of machines and exact calculation, where you used guns that might be a mile away to fire at a plane represented for you by a disturbance on a cathode ray tube. This seemed to me, and still does, the pattern of the war of the future. A man who is too squeamish to kill a rabbit can launch a rocket.

The sardonic stroke of a posting-clerk's pen that sent me to India for three years gave me one war-time experience which I should not like to have missed; close contact with South Indian gunners, who came straight to us out of the Middle Ages, with names reflecting the incarnations of the Hindu gods and with a religious tradition as closely interwoven with their lives as that of the pre-Reformation England. I wrote of these in *Indian Landscape* and worked hard to find poems that depicted India for *Poems from India*, the forces anthology I helped to edit. From India I learned something of the Middle Ages from which we came; from the world of guns and radar I learned something of that for which we seem to be bound – the world of machines and modern witchcraft to which the war introduced me.

Paul Dehn

I voted vehemently against fighting 'for King and Country' in the Oxford Union debate of 1933; as vehemently joined the Territorials (3rd Bn. London Scottish) after Munich; and at war's outbreak found myself lurking bemusedly on an Ack-Ack site in the heart of Moss Bros.' playing-fields at Eltham. After nine months of firing not a single shot in anger for a gunner's wage of two shillings a day, my Battery Commander's discovery that I spoke good French and indifferent Norwegian earned me an intriguingly non-committal interview with Peter Fleming at a discreet little office in Horse Guards; three months later at an Aldershot OCTU from which (while Dunkirk foundered) I emerged a 2nd Lieutenant in the Intelligence Corps; and one month's backbreaking attachment to the Independent Companies (later Commandos) as Lochailort, Inverness. Here I was taught to run up mountains without minding, to navigate light craft in coastal waters and to commit sabotage.

I became fully qualified to save Norway in the week after Norway had already fallen, and to save France a couple of days after France fell, too. I was therefore posted to Winchester, trained as a Field Security Officer, promoted Lieutenant and attached to 59 Div. (holding the crucial strip of coast between West Hartlepool and Scarborough) with instructions to keep the coast clear of spies.

After six months in which my FS Section and I succeeded only in securing the arrest of an old man who had shouted 'Heil Hitler!' during the playing of the National Anthem after an ENSA concert at Great Ayton – he was acquitted – I was promoted Captain and attached to Special Operations Executive (the then top-secret unit charged with organizing active resistance in all enemy-occupied territory) as an instructor to newly recruited West European saboteurs.

Guilt stung me to seriousness. From the safety of half-a-dozen pseudo-Tudor houses sequestered in the New Forest around Beaulieu, my colleagues and I (who had never been operational) had to teach men and women – French, Belgian, Norwegian, Danish, Czech, Polish and Yugoslav – to go back by parachute or sub-chaser into their own countries, to live there in unobtrusive secrecy and to commit lethal acts which might (either through their own mistakes or, worse, through ours) involve them in their own deaths.

From this point I was to be haunted by the deaths of 'students' who could be imagined to have died through my possible negligence. My colleagues and I dared not dwell too deeply in our private conversation on the guilt we all tacitly shared. Nor, for security reasons, could I confide in friends (however trusted) outside SOE. My superficial safety-valve was the false-assumed, circumscribed swagger of a cloak-and-dagger existence; my honest safety-valve, the writing of poetry.

Most of my war poems arose from a need to exorcize these shadowy fears, which were later to grow arms and legs and faces. Odette Churchill was tortured. Gregers Gram swallowed a suicide pill at the moment of arrest. The posthumous citations put on flesh.

In 1944, now a Major, I sailed back from a year's Chief Instructorship at an SOE school in Canada to whizz down France in the wake of General Patton and be operationally reunited with one of my French 'students' who was crying for joy in liberated Rennes. That made it seem worth while. I also saw and smelt my first denationalized corpses. That didn't.

My war ended in Norway when, shortly after the 1945 surrender, I was attached to an SOE mission sent to thank Milorg (the resistance organization) for all it had done. I think it was at Sauda that I saw a boy called Tor staring from outside cell-bars at the imprisoned Gestapo-man who had recently tortured him by pulling off his toe-nails. Tor sat there all day, staring, until evening when he got up and stretched himself. Somebody said 'What are you going to do now, Tor?' and he said: 'I think I will go to the movies.' In the same year I stopped staring and became a film-critic.

Gavin Ewart

I didn't enjoy the Army, although after four years at Wellington, it didn't come as much of a surprise to me. I am not, nor ever have been, sufficiently 'practical' and 'efficient' to do well at that sort of thing. My spell as an officer in a Light Anti-Aircraft Regiment, engaged on the air defence of factories and airfields in the UK was one of the dullest and most boring periods of my whole life. It is better to be bored than dead – but not much. When I went overseas (ten months in North Africa, and nearly three years in Italy), I enjoyed it a lot more. We were on port defence and by December 1943, when we arrived, the German Air Force had more or less lost interest in Italy.

This was the first time that I had ever set foot on this classical peninsula. We crossed from Bizerta to Naples (always some way 'behind the battle'). Waited at Gragnano and Castellammare; then took up duties on the local airfields – Vesuvius obligingly erupted while we were there. Later the unit was disbanded. Some unfortunates went into the infantry or tanks. I was posted to a mobile Operations Room, with which (on a motorbike) I travelled up the West Coast of Italy from Torre Annunziata to La Spezia and the German surrender. We returned to our Rear Headquarters by the Torre al Gallo, overlooking Florence. Some of the great paintings came out of hiding and were shown in Rome, below and behind Mussolini's balcony. By this time I could speak and read Italian – not very well. In May 1946: England, home and beauty. All the London girls looked very pale after the dark skins of the Mediterranean.

Writing poetry during the war was very hard. The war itself, as a subject, was too near and too big. But perhaps also a sense of military inadequacy spread itself on my feelings about my verse. As a soldier, I tried hard; and I considered it a 'just war' – it was, after all, an anti-Fascist war as well as a fight for Britain's survival; but I am just not a military person. Maclaren-Ross made capital out of his own deficiencies in his wartime stories; but this was not so easy to do in verse; nor, perhaps, did I feel like doing it. I don't consider that any 'great' poetry came out of the Second World War (except for *The Unquiet Grave* which, as I have written elsewhere, seems to me to fill the bill for anyone who is looking for 'the great war poem').

It may be that some negatives have been stored away which will be developed later. After all, David Jones published *In Parenthesis* in 1937, more than twenty years after the events he describes.

Montale's fine long poem about the 1914–18 war was not written until 1963; and this must be considered well in the running for the position of 'best poem' among his works.

The war started when I was twenty-three. When I came out of the Army I was thirty. It's quite a chunk out of a lifetime; but I was lucky. A very high percentage of my fellow Wellingtonians must have been killed, or wounded. The worst I suffered from was boredom, and I saw two new countries and learned a new language.

Roy Fuller

I was called up in April 1941 as an Ordinary Seaman in the Royal Navy. However, towards the end of my initial training I had put my name down for a somewhat mysterious course for which the qualification was School Certificate physics and mathematics, and from the drafting pool at Chatham Barracks, instead of the conventional service in a big ship and commissioning in the Executive Branch, I was sent to study at Aberdeen and Lee-on-Solent, and emerged in March or April 1942 (with the Services' gift for unlikely transmogrification – I was a lawyer in civilian life) as a radar mechanic in the Fleet Air Arm. I was then drafted to Ceylon, but before I reached there Japanese bombing had forced the Fleet back to Mombasa and I went to East Africa where I worked on radar maintenance, with the eventual rating of Petty Officer. I returned to the UK in November 1943 for commissioning. More long courses, from which I was posted to the Admiralty, first in the Department of Air Equipment and then as Technical Assistant to the Director of Naval Air Radio.

I was twenty-nine at calling-up, settled in life, and with a wife and young child. This, as well as instinct, led me to help along as much as I could the luck that kept me from angry shots (even my choice of the Navy was largely determined by archetypal memories of the disagreeableness of trench life in the First War). So that as it turned out nothing, except the non-war experience of Africa, affected me as much as the proletariatization resulting from service on the 'lower deck'. I had got to know something of working-class life in left-wing politics during my early twenties: the first part of my war service confirmed in a practical way the necessity for social revolution, not least for the middle-class intellectual. It extricated me from the great problem of the thirties – how to live and write for a class to which one didn't belong. Such extrication was obviously mainly subjective, but there is certainly a simplification and greater concreteness in the first poems I wrote after calling-up, and I think the Marxist conception of things underlies them in a less strained and dragged-in way than hitherto. My African verse is on the whole more clotted, and, of course, sometimes not about the war at all. However, the oppressed fauna and humans fitted in quite well.

The belief that a revolution must occur in English society as a result of the war had faded by the time – probably before – I was commissioned. Anyway, life as an officer, and a chair-borne one at that, did not prompt me to write any further poetry, and in those days I did not think of myself in any very practical way as a novelist.

A good job, really, that I avoided death in 1941–43. The poems I wrote then, perhaps because of the very standpoint that gives them some virtue, range over experience less freely and subtly than those of Douglas and Lewis. But I think war service exorcized several evils that might have gone on constricting me as a poet. In Caudwell's term, it exchanged reality for illusion, and after the war, following an awkward period of adjustment, I was able to write verse of rather wider scope.

Bernard Gutteridge

From November of 1939 to the following spring I was a private soldier in what is now the Royal Hampshire Regiment. I was commissioned into it in '40. I was stationed in England for a year; then in Scotland training in Combined Operations. I was in the Brigade which assaulted and captured Madagascar, commanding a platoon, in 1942. Some weeks of gaiety in South Africa; then a camp outside Poona. After training there and in the Central Provinces, 36 Division (I was now at Divisional HQ) went into action in Burma on the Arakan front. We were pulled out and flown into Northern Burma in June '44 just as the Second Front opened in Europe. Here we were under command of the Americans – General Stillwell and then General Sultan. We fought our way down to south of Mandalay, supplied by air. We were flown out to prepare for the Malayan landings. But the war stopped one day and not long after I went home. I was then a a Major, G2 in 36 Division.

I wrote poems in most of those places. It was, I think, like keeping a diary. I wrote them more because I felt I ought to. I had been very excited about writing poetry in the thirties; and seeing it published. But it was not like that any more. In fact I sent no poetry to any editor until '44 when John Lehmann and Cyril Connolly published some in *Penguin New Writing* and *Horizon*. I saw none of the poets I had known before the war; kept in touch only with Geoffrey Grigson, who wrote long, kind, interesting letters. I met a new poet – Alun Lewis – and knew him only for a few weeks. With him I could talk poetry and poetry in war time (he had some wonderful letters from Robert Graves which we read together). I was a few hundred yards away along the Mayu Range when he died there in March '44.

When the war began, like all of us I expected to be pitched fairly quickly into trench warfare. With memories of the poetry of the Somme, there seemed little point in writing about blowing up rubber boats on Laffens Plain. I wrote about my brother officers and their girls, and my girls. Stupidly, I now think, I discarded all this kind of poem when Routledge published a book of my poetry just after the war. Again, I do feel that many of my poems about being in action, about the fighting, show signs of someone saying: you are a poet and occasionally in action. Write about it. I was perhaps more myself on Johannesburg and Bombay racecourses.

I don't know that my poems say much about my *attitude* to the war. I spent the most exciting part of my war in a Division led and manned by most delightful people. My attitude was one of thankfulness that I was with them. Two poems simply reflect the gay efficiency of the 2nd Battalion The Royal Welch Fusiliers, from Colonel Gwydr' down. South Africa, Madagascar, India, Burma – they are thrilling places to go to when you are young and have a pretty free run of them. To find that the war *you yourself* were in was not like the one Owen and Sorley wrote about (nor the one the Chindits fought or the infantry) led more to slap-and-tickle verse than war poetry.

H. B. Mallalieu

I served in the Royal Artillery from 1940 to 1946, taking part in the Sicily landing and the Italian campaign and serving subsequently in Greece and Austria. Looking back on the poems I wrote during this period I notice that they are less didactic, less concerned with abstract ideas, less political than the pre-war poems. People, things, relationships and individual experience became more significant for me personally because their ephemeral nature was so continuously and consistently made apparent in the war years. I think, like most poets of that time, I regretted that we were being called upon to fight against something we regarded as wrong without, at the same time, having the conviction that we were defending a way of life that was right. But the necessity of war was accepted and if the challenge was not accepted with the jubilation that Rupert Brooke had shown a generation earlier, it was seen as inevitable. The attitude of opposition, which dominated the poetry of the thirties, was no longer fitting; scarcely even possible. Because there was no illusion at the outset, there was not subsequent outcry against the futility of war, or the mismanagement of it, as there had been in the First World War.

The battle for which as soldiers we were being trained or in which we fought took the place – in my case at least – of a god in which we did not believe or of a Communist Utopia in which most of us had already ceased to have faith. But whereas I had written poems inspired by the Spanish Civil War, in which I did not participate, and would no doubt have written fervently as a Christian if I had then been one in war time it seemed to be the incidental things that mattered. One was trying to stop the bullet in its flight, trying to leave an imprint in the air. In writing I was defending those things which above all, nostalgia had given a perhaps inflated value. My poems were, I think, at best what used to be called occasional. They reflect a period rather than an individual talent.

F. T. Prince

I cannot consider myself a war-poet. Though I spent more than five years in uniform, I never came near any fighting, and the worst trials and dangers I encountered were those faced by the civilian population in Southern England in 1940–41 and 1944–45. Yet the war years were important to me for the new experiences they brought, of a kind which I should never have had in peacetime. Army training, and some months of regimental life, forced me to the discovery that I could do many practical tasks – also to the discovery of other people whose lives one could share. I saw more of English life and English character than I had ever seen before, and saw it more from within, since I had never known before such a sense of 'belonging' of being a functioning part of the general life. If this was an experience shared by almost everyone else who was young and actively involved, it was nevertheless especially important to me, since I had been an 'outsider' by birth and education.

The effect of the war and of those new experiences on my

poetry seems to me to have been almost wholly bad, while they lasted. The forms in which I had tried to write, and sometimes succeeded, before the war were quite inadequate, or at least unsuited, to even my modified experience of the war. Perhaps my poetry was too reflective and concentrated, and needed time and thought and a margin for experiment and error: it could not become a notation of day-by-day experience. I wrote little, and was not satisfied with any of it. But the reason was that I was experiencing too much, learning too much, developing too much, and I can only hope that the poetry I have written since the war has not been unworthy of all the new experiences and emotions that the war involved me in.

John Pudney

I began my war service in 1939 on the water, as a member of the crew of A. P. Herbert's *Water Gipsy*. A shipmate was Victor Pasmore. When we were not afloat we were billeted in the cellars at Lambeth Palace. The following year I joined the Royal Air Force, was trained as an intelligence officer and posted to Coastal Command. I was later transferred to a special Public Relations branch partly concerned with the writing of books in association with the late Hilary St George Saunders. But there were also special assignments which took me during the course of the war to Iceland, North and South America, West and Equatorial Africa, Sudan, Middle East, Malta, Greece, Yugoslavia. During the Normandy campaign I was 'special observer', sometimes working with the Americans, sometimes with the French. From about 1942 I was very rarely in Britain.

The effects of war and constant movement on my writing stimulated verse. Certain experiences, sometimes shared, sometimes merely observed, could only be expressed in the economical and imaginative terms of poetry. I am aware now that there was a degree of over-simplification. War is infinitely more simple than peace, though not the least admirable on that score.

Alan Ross

I joined the Navy on my twentieth birthday, straight from Oxford. My initial training was done at a Butlin's Camp at Skegness, about which I can only remember the cold, the loneliness of being the only non-Geordie in a Tyneside draft, some horrifying lectures on VD, and the Divisional Officer saying that by the number of French Letters lying around the streets they must be growing on trees.

From Skegness I went to a Fleet Air Arm station at Lee-on-Solent, where my course was interrupted by a priority call from the Admiralty who wanted anyone who could speak German. It saved my bacon, for my squadron was later eliminated in a suicidal attack on the *Scharnhorst*.

I spent several months at Wimbledon, mugging up German codes and learning to decipher complicated signals which were usually changed before we had time to use them.

In December 1942 I was drafted as an Ordinary Seaman to *Onslow*, a Fleet destroyer then at Scapa Flow. We sailed immediately for Murmansk, picking up a large convoy off Iceland. A week out we were attacked by the *Hipper* and the *Lützow*, in company with a swarm of German destroyers. We suffered a lot of damage and many casualties, limping into Murmansk with a grotesque list. *Onslow* was in dock for the rest of the winter and the crew dispersed. I was transferred to a minesweeper and we were pestered by U-boats all the way back. It was a very rough period.

Eventually I joined another destroyer, the *Vivien*, escorting convoys from Rosyth via E-boat Alley to Sheerness. I became a Leading Seaman and enjoyed myself. We had a night's action on the way down and another on the way back and you could set your watch by our progress. I left *Vivien* to be commissioned, returning to Harwich as Assistant Intelligence Officer on the staff of Captain (D), 19th Destroyer Flotilla. For the rest of the war I sailed in a variety of destroyers and frigates, our main job being to break up attacks on convoys made by E-boats and one-man torpedoes. We were fairly frequently in action and it was all exciting rather than frightening, and hardly ever boring. I was selfishly sorry when it came to an end, because I had no idea what I should do, having no degree and no money. I went to Wilhelmshaven for a year, working nominally on the de-nazification of the German Navy, but doing a good deal of interpreting and other Intelligence chores besides. I was demobilized in 1947, by which time Oxford – where I had been a contemporary at St John's of Philip Larkin, Kingsley Amis and Edward du Cann – seemed too remote a place to return to.

The Navy – at least when one was at sea – was ideal for writing, once you got used to the noise and complete lack of privacy. Also for reading: I think I must have read and re-read between 1942 and 1945 almost every volume of poetry published since Eliot's first book, hundreds of American novels, the complete works of D. H. Lawrence, Forster, Isherwood, Green and Greene among others.

I felt a week was wasted that produced no poem. Out of a hundred or so I've kept a dozen, though many others appeared in magazines. The issues of the war seemed to me clear beyond all ambiguity, therefore one could concentrate on recording a kind of existence as accurately as possible. I had no particular ties, no important relationships, so deprivation or separation were not the motivating impulses they were for others, and have since been for me. I found the sea beautiful and life in a warship rich and rewarding. I hoped to survive, so I could live the romance I had read about. That's about all there was to it, though since there was virtually no sea-war poetry in either war I found making my own poems unusually difficult. Had the war come a bit later I might have been able to do better by it.

Julian Symons

I was conscripted in April, 1942, and I served as a trooper in the RAC until 1944, when I was invalided out because of an arm injury, not sustained through enemy action. As to my 'attitude to the war', I think that, rather than using hindsight about this, it's better to repeat something I wrote at the time, in answer to a question about 'Poetry and the War':

'I don't believe that the "war poet" exists. All poets are war poets, and peace poets too. It is pointless to "demand" of poets in this or perhaps in any war any degree of participation or support of one side or another. Most of the best lyrics have been written a long way from the battlefield. It is a truism just worth repeating that the preservation of individual integrity is an important thing for the poet; and an interest in humanity is another important thing. If our poets were more interested in men, and less in themselves, we might have had some better war poems.

'But these are only minor and partial illuminations because, I believe, the question does not permit serious treatment. Questions about "poetry and the war" are still basically questions about the position of the writer in capitalist society. So perhaps I should say merely that two years spent in the Army gave me feelings of comradship which it is difficult for the petty bourgeois intellectual to feel except in such conditions; and gave me also the most bitter contempt and distaste for the bureaucracy and class distinction with which the British Army is permeated.

'In the Army I had the useful experience of seeing this bureaucracy and class distinction from the bottom of the social scale; in civilian life I'm halfway up it. These two feelings, of comradeship and bitterness, I've tried to put into some poems.' (1944)

Richard Eberhart

Of the several war poems I wrote during the Second World War 'The Fury of Aerial Bombardment' has been most studied, and perhaps it is enough for me to say a few words about that poem. It was written in Dam Neck, Virginia, in the summer of 1944 while I as stationed there as a Naval Reserve officer teaching aerial free gunnery. I taught tens of thousands of young Americans to shoot the .50 calibre Browning machine gun from aircraft. The subject was called Sighting. All too soon their names would come back in the death lists. This depressed me so much that one time I was sitting on a barracks steps at the end of the day and felt the ruthlessness and senselessness of war so acutely that I wrote the first three stanzes of the poem, which are in effect a kind of prayer. I put it away. Sometime later I felt it needed something added to it. Maybe the interval was a week or two. With an analytical mind, quite removed from the passionate one of the first three stanzas, I composed the last four lines. It is said that these in relation to the others make this a particularly modern poem. Indeed, if I had not added the last stanzas, perhaps the poem would remain unused.

Louis Simpson

I enlisted in the US Army in 1943. A year later I was assigned to a glider-infantry regiment of the 101st Airborne Division, stationed in Britain, I served with the 101st in France, Holland, Belgium, and Germany. In combat I was a runner – that is, I carried messages. In Holland I was wounded by a shell fragment, and at Bastogne my feet were frost-bitten. I got through the war all right, but afterwards, when I was back in the States, I had a 'nervous breakdown' and was hospitalized. I had amnesia; the war was blacked out in my mind, and so were episodes of my life before the war. When I left the hospital I found that I could hardly read or write. In these circumstances I began writing poems.

Before the war I had written a few poems and some prose. Now

I found that poetry was the only kind of writing in which I could express my thoughts. Through poems I could release the irrational. grotesque images I had accumulated during the war; and imposing order on these images enabled me to recover my identity. In 1948, when I was living in Paris, one night I dreamed that I was lying on the bank of a canal, under machine gun and mortar fire. The next morning I wrote it out, in the poem 'Carentan O Carentan', and as I wrote I realized that it wasn't a dream, but the memory of my first time under fire. So I began piecing the war together, and wrote other poems. 'Memories of a Lost War' describes the early days of the fighting in Normandy; 'The Battle', the fighting at Bastogne.

Twelve years after the war I wrote a long poem, 'The Runner', which was devoted to the dog-face soldier's war. I wanted to represent the drudgery of that life, the numbing of intellect and emotion, and the endurance of the American infantry soldier. I wanted to write a poem that would be abrasive, like a pebble in a shoe. Some readers thought this flat poem a mistake, but other readers, who were infantrymen, appreciated the details. To a foot-soldier, war is almost entirely physical. That is why some men, when they think about war, fall silent. Language seems to falsify physical life and to betray those who have experienced it absolutely – the dead. As Hemingway remarked, to such men the names on a map are more significant than works of imagination.

However, in a post-war world there are limitations to the dog-face way of looking at things. Love, for example, is not best written about by a man who is trying to avoid extra duty. And a country cannot be governed by silence and inertia. In recent years the close-mouthed, almost sullen, manner of my early poems has given way to qualities that are quite different. Like other men of the war generation, I began with middle age; youth came later. Nowadays in my poems I try to generate mystery and excitement; I have even dealt in general ideas. But I retain the dog-face's suspicion of the officer class, with their abstract language and indifference to individual, human suffering. You might say that the war made me a foot-soldier for the rest of my life.

What, in these poems, was I trying to do that had not already been done? I did not wish to protest against war. Any true description of modern warfare is a protest, but many have written against war with satire or indignation, and it still goes on. My object was to remember. I wished to show the war exactly, as though I were painting a landscape or a face. I wanted people to find in my poems the truth of what it had been like to be an

American infantry soldier. Now I see that I was writing a memorial of those years, for the men I had known, who were silent. I was trying to write poems that I would not be ashamed to have them read – poems that would be, in their laconic and simple manner, tolerable to men who had seen a good deal of combat and had no illusions.

Select Bibliography

(Only volumes of war-time verse and subsequent Collected editions are listed)

Drummond Allison: *The Yellow Night* (Fortune Press, 1944)

Jocelyn Brooke: *December Spring* (Bodley Head, 1946)

Norman Cameron: *Work in Hand* (Hogarth Press, 1942)

Roy Campbell: *Talking Bronco* (Faber and Faber, 1940)
Collected Poems (The Bodley Head, 1957)

Charles Causley: *Farewell Aggie Weston* (Hand and Flower Press, 1951)
Survivor's Leave (Hand and Flower Press, 1953)
Union Street (Rupert Hart-Davis, 1957)

Herbert Corby: *Hampdens Going Over* (Editions Poetry London, 1945)
Time in a Blue Prison (Fortune Press, 1947)

R. N. Currey: *This Other Planet* (Routledge, 1945)
Indian Landscape (Routledge, 1947)

Keith Douglas: *Alamein to Zem Zem* (Prose. Editions Poetry London, 1946)
Collected Poems (Editions Poetry London, 1951)
Selected Poems (ed. Ted Hughes. Faber and Faber, 1964)

Roy Fuller: *The Middle of a War* (Hogarth Press, 1942)
A Lost Season (Hogarth Press, 1944)
Collected Poems (Andre Deutsch, 1962)

Richard Eberhart: *Collected Poems* (Chatto and Windus, 1960)

Bernard Gutteridge: *Traveller's Eye* (Routledge, 1947)

Hamish Henderson: *Elegies for the dead in Cyrenaica* (John Lehmann, 1948)

Randall Jarrell: *Blood for a Stranger* (Harcourt Brace, NY, 1942)
Little Friend, Little Friend (Dial Press, NY, 1948)

Sidney Keyes: *Collected Poems* (Routledge, 1945)

Alun Lewis: *Raiders' Dawn* (Allen and Unwin, 1942)
Ha! Ha! Among the Trumpets (Allen and Unwin, 1944)

Howard Nemerov: *The Image and the Law* (Holt, NY, 1947)

F. T. Prince: *Soldiers Bathing* (Fortune Press, 1954)

	The Doors of Stone (Rupert Hart-Davis, 1963)
Henry Reed:	*A Map of Verona* (Jonathan Cape, 1946)
Alan Ross:	*Something of the Sea* (Verschoyle, 1954)
	To Whom it may Concern (Hamish Hamilton, 1958)
Julian Symons:	*The Second Man* (Routledge, 1943)
Richard Wilbur:	*Poems 1943–56* (Faber and Faber, 1957)

NEL BESTSELLERS

Crime

T013 332	CLOUDS OF WITNESS	Dorothy L. Sayers	40p
W002 871	THE UNPLEASANTNESS AT THE BELLONA CLUB	Dorothy L. Sayers	30p
W003 011	GAUDY NIGHT	Dorothy L. Sayers	40p
T010 457	THE NINE TAILORS	Dorothy L. Sayers	35p
T012 484	FIVE RED HERRINGS	Dorothy L. Sayers	40p
T012 492	UNNATURAL DEATH	Dorothy L. Sayers	40p

Fiction

W002 775	HATTER'S CASTLE	A. J. Cronin	60p
W002 777	THE STARS LOOK DOWN	A. J. Cronin	60p
T010 414	THE CITADEL	A. J. Cronin	60p
T010 422	THE KEYS OF THE KINGDOM	A. J. Cronin	50p
T001 288	THE TROUBLE WITH LAZY ETHEL	Ernest K. Gann	30p
T003 922	IN THE COMPANY OF EAGLES	Ernest K. Gann	30p
W002 145	THE NINTH DIRECTIVE	Adam Hall	25p
T012 271	THE WARSAW DOCUMENT	Adam Hall	40p
T011 305	THE STRIKER PORTFOLIO	Adam Hall	30p
T007 243	SYLVIA SCARLETT	Compton Mackenzie	30p
T007 669	SYLVIA AND ARTHUR	Compton Mackenzie	30p
T007 677	SYLVIA AND MICHAEL	Compton Mackenzie	35p
W002 772	TO THE CORAL STRAND	John Masters	40p
W002 788	TRIAL AT MONOMOY	John Masters	40p
T009 084	SIR, YOU BASTARD	G. F. Newman	30p
T012 522	THURSDAY MY LOVE	Robert H. Rimmer	40p
T009 769	THE HARRAD EXPERIMENT	Robert H. Rimmer	40p
T010 252	THE REBELLION OF YALE MARRATT	Robert H. Rimmer	40p
T010 716	THE ZOLOTOV AFFAIR	Robert H. Rimmer	30p
T013 820	THE DREAM MERCHANTS	Harold Robbins	75p
W002 783	79 PARK AVENUE	Harold Robbins	50p
T012 255	THE CARPETBAGGERS	Harold Robbins	80p
T011 801	WHERE LOVE HAS GONE	Harold Robbins	70p
T013 707	THE ADVENTURERS	Harold Robbins	80p
T006 743	THE INHERITORS	Harold Robbins	60p
T009 467	STILETTO	Harold Robbins	30p
T010 406	NEVER LEAVE ME	Harold Robbins	30p
T011 771	NEVER LOVE A STRANGER	Harold Robbins	70p
T011 798	A STONE FOR DANNY FISHER	Harold Robbins	60p
T011 461	THE BETSY	Harold Robbins	75p
T010 201	RICH MAN, POOR MAN	Irwin Shaw	80p
W002 186	THE PLOT	Irving Wallace	75p
W002 761	THE SEVEN MINUTES	Irving Wallace	75p
T009 718	THE THREE SIRENS	Irving Wallace	75p
T010 341	THE PRIZE	Irving Wallace	80p

Historical

T009 750	THE WARWICK HEIRESS	Margaret Abbey	30p
T011 607	THE SON OF YORK	Margaret Abbey	30p
T011 585	THE ROSE IN SPRING	Eleanor Fairburn	30p
T009 734	RICHMOND AND ELIZABETH	Brenda Honeyman	30p
T011 593	HARRY THE KING	Brenda Honeyman	35p
T009 742	THE ROSE BOTH RED AND WHITE	Betty King	30p
W002 479	AN ODOUR OF SANCTITY	Frank Yerby	50p
W002 824	THE FOXES OF HARROW	Frank Yerby	50p
W002 916	BENTON'S ROW	Frank Yerby	40p
W003 010	THE VIXENS	Frank Yerby	40p
T006 921	JARRETT'S JADE	Frank Yerby	40p
T010 988	BRIDE OF LIBERTY	Frank Yerby	30p

Science Fiction

T007 081	THE CANOPY OF TIME	Brian Aldiss	30p
W003 003	CARSON OF VENUS	Edgar Rice Burroughs	30p
W002 449	THE MOON IS A HARSH MISTRESS	Robert Heinlein	40p
W002 697	THE WORLDS OF ROBERT HEINLEIN	Robert Heinlein	25p
W002 839	SPACE FAMILY STONE	Robert Heinlein	30p
W002 844	STRANGER IN A STRANGE LAND	Robert Heinlein	60p

T006	778	ASSIGNMENT IN ETERNITY	Robert Heinlein	25p
T007	294	HAVE SPACESUIT – WILL TRAVEL	Robert Heinlein	30p
T009	696	GLORY ROAD	Robert Heinlein	40p
T011	844	DUNE	Frank Herbert	75p
T012	298	DUNE MESSIAH	Frank Herbert	40p
W002	814	THE WORLDS OF FRANK HERBERT	Frank Herbert	30p
W002	911	SANTAROGA BARRIER	Frank Herbert	30p
W003	001	DRAGON IN THE SEA	Frank Herbert	30p

War

W002	921	WOLF PACK	William Hardy	30p
W002	484	THE FLEET THAT HAD TO DIE	Richard Hough	25p
W002	805	HUNTING OF FORCE Z	Richard Hough	30p
W002	632	THE BASTARD BRIGADE	Peter Leslie	25p
T006	999	KILLER CORPS	Peter Leslie	25p
T011	755	TRAWLERS GO TO WAR	Lund and Ludlam	40p
W005	051	GOERING	Manvell & Freankel	52½p
W005	065	HIMMLER	Manvell & Freankel	52½p
W002	423	STRIKE FROM THE SKY	Alexander McKee	30p
W002	831	NIGHT	Francis Pollini	40p
T010	074	THE GREEN BERET	Hilary St. George Saunders	40p
T010	066	THE RED BERET	Hilary St. George Saunders	40p

Western

T010	619	EDGE – THE LONER	George Gilman	25p
T010	600	EDGE – TEN THOUSAND DOLLARS AMERICAN	George Gilman	25p
T010	929	EDGE – APACHE DEATH	George Gilman	25p

General

T011	763	SEX MANNERS FOR MEN	Robert Chartham	30p
W002	531	SEX MANNERS FOR ADVANCED LOVERS	Robert Chartham	25p
W002	835	SEX AND THE OVER FORTIES	Robert Chartham	30p
T010	732	THE SENSUOUS COUPLE	Dr. C.	25p
P002	367	AN ABZ OF LOVE	Inge and Sten Hegeler	60p
P011	402	A HAPPIER SEX LIFE	Dr. Sha Kokken	70p
W002	584	SEX MANNERS FOR SINGLE GIRLS	Georges Valensin	25p
W002	592	THE FRENCH ART OF SEX MANNERS	Georges Valensin	25p
W002	726	THE POWER TO LOVE	E. W. Hirsch M. D.	47½p

Mad

S003	491	LIKE MAD		30p
S003	494	MAD IN ORBIT		30p
S003	520	THE BEDSIDE MAD		30p
S003	521	THE VOODOO MAD		30p
S003	657	MAD FOR BETTER OR VERSE		30p
S003	716	THE SELF MADE MAD		30p

— — — — — — — — — — — — — —

NEL P.O. BOX 11, FALMOUTH, CORNWALL

Please send cheque or postal order. Allow 6p per book to cover postage and packing.

Name..

Address ....

....

Title ....
(SEPTEMBER)